ASIAN
VEGETARIAN COOKING

by Thidavadee Camsong and Peter Lüffe

Photography by Heinz-Josef Beckers

BARRON'S

TABLE OF CONTENTS

Simple, Tasty, Healthy

These three words succinctly describe vegetarian cooking. Asia, which boasts a vegetarian tradition that is more than three thousand years old, proves how multifaceted the vegetarian cuisine can be.

Whatever country in Asia you visit, the wealth of fruit and vegetables, the variety of food, and the loving care with which the food is prepared will overwhelm you. Of course, the cuisines of the different regions vary according to their geographical and climatic conditions, the composition of the population, and religious and secular traditions.

In **China**, there is a saying "Anyone who eats well-balanced is well-balanced," meaning that the food passes the palate and stomach and goes to the center of the body: the soul. Dishes are combined according to the yin-yang principle that rules all Chinese life. Warm foods prepared according to yang, the masculine principle, are served with cool foods belonging to yin, the feminine principle; sweet with salty, soft with firm, mild with sharp.

Chopsticks are used throughout China. Bite-size morsels of food are picked up with the paired tips; larger pieces of food can be divided with the chopsticks. Large, firm pieces of food, too big to be eaten in one bite, are picked up with chopsticks, a piece is bitten off, and the remaining bite is returned to the plate. Rice is eaten directly from the bowl, with the help of chopsticks. The bowl is lifted to the chin with the left hand, and the rice is pushed into the mouth with the chopsticks in the right hand.

Indonesia is a republic with many ethnic groups, and the cuisine of the country varies accordingly. The influences come from India, China, and Holland. Traditionally, the food is cut into bite-size bits, served on plates or banana leaves, then eaten with a spoon and fork. The fork is used to push food onto the spoon; the spoon is the actual eating utensil. Knives ordinarily are not used as eating utensils.

The cuisine of **Japan** is characterized by Buddhism and Shintoism, the oldest religions in the country. While the food is being prepared, great care is taken to retain the natural flavors of each food item. Seasoning is done very carefully in Japan. In this respect, the Japanese cuisine varies greatly from that of Southeast Asia, in which hot curry pastes and chile peppers dictate the focus of the palate. Besides retaining the natural flavors of food, Japanese cuisine has another typical characteristic: The food is aesthetically pleasing. A Japanese meal not only is a pleasure for the palate, but also a delight to the eyes.

In **Thailand**, as in China, the individual dishes of a meal also are finely balanced. The center of any meal is a large bowl of rice, around which a variety of roasted, steamed, broiled, boiled, and stir-fried items are offered. The cuisine emphasizes the contrasts of sweet and salty, mild and hot, as well as the variety of cooking methods. As in Indonesia, eating is done with a spoon and fork, except with noodle dishes, which usually are prepared in the Chinese manner, and soups. Chopsticks are used to eat noodles, and soup is drunk directly from the bowl.

The cuisine of **Vietnam** varies with its different Asian influences, but is most strongly influenced by China. The basic foods are the same as those in China and Thailand, with rice at the center. About two thousand varieties of rice are said to be grown in Vietnam. The most popular variety is long-grain rice, which is boiled in plain water. Food is eaten with chopsticks, with emphasis on the skillful handling of the utensils.

Basic Ingredients for Asian Cuisine

bamboo shoots (canned)
chili powder
garlic
ginger*
coconut milk (canned)
dried mu-err mushrooms*
dried shiitake mushrooms*
light and dark soy sauces*
mirin*
palm sugar* (can substitute brown sugar)
sesame oil*
su*
tamarind* (after being opened, keeps 3 months in refrigerator)

Can be frozen:
chile peppers
ginger*
lemon leaves* (kaffir lime leaves)
lemongrass*

Items that are marked with *, here and in the recipes, are described in the glossary in the back of the book.

Special Note
The recipes in this cookbook sometimes list salt as an ingredient, with no quantity given. This way, the cook can salt to taste. The salt quantity used to create the nutritional charts for each recipe is $1/8$ teaspoon.

5

SATISFYING
STAPLE

Soups

What would Asian cuisine be without soup? Devoid of delicate dishes, at the least. Soups are an important part of mealtime in Asia, and there are numerous recipes for every taste, from very mild to fiery hot.

From Morning to Evening

For many Asians, the day begins with soup: Boiled rice is warmed in a vegetable broth, then seasoned with cilantro, grated garlic, or other seasonings.

Freshly prepared soups are sold round the clock by street vendors and in large stores. All, except noodle soups, are served with boiled rice.

Soups generally are served not as an appetizer but "right smack in the middle" of the meal. During an Asian meal, all the dishes come to the table at the same time, including several varieties of soup. This allows the different taste sensations to complement one another; a mild soup is used to soothe the tongue after a hot taste or conversely, after a spoonful of spicy soup, a less strongly seasoned dish provides balance.

The Basis

The basis for all vegetarian soups is a clear, flavorful vegetable broth (page 9). Depending on the dish, you can season this basic broth even more with mirin, soy sauce, or sesame oil. Take care that the broth doesn't have too intense a flavor to begin with, since you will be adding spicy ingredients to it.

It's best to prepare a large quantity of broth at one time. Freeze in portions what you don't plan to use immediately. Vegetable broth keeps in the freezer for about three months.

Fast Versions

To cut your preparation time when making soup, you can use instant or canned vegetable broth instead of homemade. When making instant broth, dissolve the granules in hot water according to the directions on the package. As a rule, vegetable broth is not thickened, but it occasionally is made creamy with coconut milk in some soup recipes.

Hot Seasoning

Some soups are so hot that they literally take your breath away. If this is not to your liking, you can either use fewer chilies than the recipe calls for, or you can remove the seeds. The seeds contain capsaicin, the component that gives chilies their fiery heat.

When working with chilies, it's best to wear gloves. Avoid getting your fingers near your eyes, since they will really burn. Wash your hands after working with chilies. If you plan to mash chilies in the mortar, cover the top so that juice doesn't spray into your eyes.

Invite Friends in to Share

A good way to experience the variety of Asian soups is a Sunday soup brunch. Choose a variety of soups from each of the five countries featured in this book. For example:

Won Ton Soup from China (page 20)
Spinach Soup from Indonesia (page 20)
Noodle Soup from Japan (page 18)
Oyster Mushroom Soup from Thailand (page 12)
Dark Vegetable Soup from Vietnam (page 10)

Serve the soups with plenty of hot rice, and sample and enjoy them together with your family and friends.

Basic Vegetable Broth

For 2¹/₂ quarts (2.5 l) broth, you need about 8³/₄ oz (250 g) celery, 8³/₄ oz (250 g) carrots, 7 oz (200 g) daikon radish, and 2 medium-size leeks. Trim, wash, and cut vegetables into coarse pieces. To give broth more flavor and color, peel 2 onions, halve them, and roast them until black on a hot stove burner. Put all these ingredients in a large pot with 3 quarts (3 l) water. Season with several washed sprigs of cilantro, 2 peeled garlic cloves, 1 bay leaf, 2 whole cloves, 10 black peppercorns, and salt. Let the broth simmer, loosely covered, for about 45 minutes. Strain through a fine sieve, discarding solids.

Mixed Vegetable Soup

1 small cauliflower
(about 1$\frac{1}{8}$ lb/500 g)
$\frac{2}{3}$ lb (300 g) broccoli
2 medium-size carrots
$\frac{2}{3}$ lb (300 g) Chinese cabbage
1 medium-size leek
2 bunches cilantro*
5 garlic cloves
$\frac{2}{3}$ lb (300 g) firm tofu
$\frac{5}{8}$ cup (150 ml) vegetable oil
2 quarts (2 l) vegetable broth
(see page 9)
scant $\frac{1}{4}$ cup (45 ml) light soy
sauce*
2 tablespoons dark soy sauce*
2 tablespoons palm sugar*
2 teaspoons salt

Preparation time:
about 45 minutes

Dark Vegetable Soup

$\frac{2}{3}$ lb (300 g) daikon radish
2 large carrots
about $\frac{1}{2}$ lb (200 g) Chinese
cabbage
5 garlic cloves
generous $\frac{1}{4}$ cup (75 ml)
vegetable oil
scant $\frac{1}{4}$ cup (45 ml) teriyaki
sauce
2 tablespoons sugar
1 teaspoon salt
$\frac{1}{2}$ teaspoon freshly ground
black pepper
1 quart (1 l) vegetable broth
(see page 9)

Preparation time:
about 35 minutes

10

Mixed Vegetable Soup
From Thailand • Pictured

• Wash the vegetables, trim, and cut into bite-size pieces.

• Wash the cilantro and remove the roots. Chop cilantro stems and leaves coarsely. Peel garlic and mash in the mortar along with the cilantro roots.

• Cut the tofu into strips. Heat $\frac{1}{2}$ cup oil in a wok over high heat. Add tofu and fry until golden, about 5 minutes; remove tofu with a slotted spoon, and drain on paper towels.

• Bring the vegetable broth to a boil in a large pot. Add the garlic-cilantro paste to the remaining oil in the wok and fry until golden. Add the cauliflower, broccoli, and carrots, and fry over high heat for about 1 minute. Add the Chinese cabbage, leek, soy sauces, palm sugar, and salt. Fry about 1 minute more.

• Remove the vegetable mixture with a slotted spoon and add to the broth; boil over medium heat for about 10 minutes. Season to taste with salt.

Makes 6 servings.

PER SERVING:	351 CALORIES	
NUTRITIONAL INFORMATION		
Carbohydrate 21		g
Protein 12		g
Total fat 27		g
Cholesterol 0		mg
Sodium 3182		mg
Fiber 3		g

Dark Vegetable Soup
From Vietnam • Easy to prepare

• Peel the radish and carrots, and cut into $\frac{1}{8}$-inch- ($\frac{1}{2}$-cm)- thick slices. Trim the Chinese cabbage. Remove the individual leaves, wash, and chop coarsely.

• Peel and mince the garlic. Heat the oil in a large, deep pan over high heat. Add the garlic and fry until it is golden. Add the daikon radish and carrots, and fry for about 3 minutes. Add the Chinese cabbage, teriyaki sauce, sugar, salt, and pepper, and fry about 2 more minutes.

• Add the broth to the vegetables and let boil for about 15 minutes. Season the soup to taste with sugar and salt.

Makes 6 servings.

Variations
You also can prepare this soup with kohlrabi or cauliflower.

PER SERVING:	145 CALORIES	
NUTRITIONAL INFORMATION		
Carbohydrate 13		g
Protein 3		g
Total fat 10		g
Cholesterol 0		mg
Sodium 1767		mg
Fiber 2		g

Yellow Vegetable Soup

1 piece pumpkin
(about 1 lb/400 g)
2 large carrots
4 medium-size potatoes
8 shallots
2 red chilies
3 kemiri nuts*
1 stalk lemongrass*
1 (2-inch) piece fresh ginger*
1 quart (1 l) vegetable broth
(see page 9)
1 teaspoon turmeric*
1 pinch laos*
2 Indian bay leaves* (salam)
1²/₃ cups (400 ml) coconut
milk
1 teaspoon salt

Preparation time:
about 40 minutes

Oyster Mushroom Soup

1¹/₈ lb (500 g) oyster
mushrooms
3 stalks lemongrass*
1 (2-inch) piece galangal*
6 lemon leaves* (kaffir lime)
2 bunches cilantro*
2 tablespoons vegetable oil
5 large dried chilies
3¹/₃ cups (800 ml) coconut
milk
¹/₄ cup (60 ml) light soy sauce*
¹/₂ teaspoon salt
4 tablespoons lime juice

Preparation time:
about 30 minutes

Yellow Vegetable Soup

From Indonesia • Pictured

• Peel the pumpkin, carrots, and potatoes, and cut into bite-size pieces. Peel the shallots and chop fine. Wash the chilies and remove the stems.

• Finely mash the shallots, kemiri nuts, and chilies in a mortar. Wash the lemongrass and chop very fine. Peel and finely chop the ginger.

• Bring the vegetable broth to a boil, and add the shallot-chile paste, lemongrass, ginger, turmeric, laos, and Indian bay leaves. Let boil for about 1 minute.

• Add the pumpkin, carrots, and potatoes to the broth, and cook over low heat for about 20 minutes. Stir in coconut milk and salt. Let boil for about 3 more minutes.

Makes 4 servings.

Oyster Mushroom Soup

From Thailand • Refreshing

• Wash the oyster mushrooms, remove and discard the tough ends, then tear mushrooms into large pieces. Wash the lemongrass and cut into 2-inch- (5-cm)-long pieces; crush with a heavy knife.

• Wash and crush the galangal. Wash the lime leaves and cut into quarters. Wash the cilantro and remove roots; chop leaves and stems coarsely and set aside. Heat the oil in a frying pan over medium heat. Add the chilies and fry for about 2 minutes, then set them to one side.

• Heat the coconut milk in a pot over medium heat. Add oyster mushrooms, lemongrass, galangal, and lime leaves. Let simmer, uncovered, over low heat for about 3 minutes. Season with soy sauce, salt, and lime juice.

• Divide soup among 4 bowls. Coarsely chop chilies, then sprinkle over the soup, along with the cilantro.

Makes 4 servings.

PER SERVING:	498 CALORIES	
NUTRITIONAL INFORMATION		
Carbohydrate	63	g
Protein	10	g
Total fat	27	g
Cholesterol	0	mg
Sodium	1621	mg
Fiber	8	g

PER SERVING:	595 CALORIES	
NUTRITIONAL INFORMATION		
Carbohydrate	21	g
Protein	11	g
Total fat	56	g
Cholesterol	0	mg
Sodium	1366	mg
Fiber	8	g

Soup of Mixed Mushrooms

From Vietnam • Pictured

• Soak the shiitake mushrooms in warm water for about 20 minutes. Meanwhile, wash oyster and button mushrooms, trim, and chop into bite-size pieces. Drain shiitake mushrooms in a colander and press out any extra water; halve them, removing any hard spots.

• Peel and finely chop the ginger and garlic. Wash the cilantro, and remove the roots. Finely chop the roots; coarsely chop the stems and leaves. Set aside. In a small bowl, combine cornmeal with 4 tablespoons of water and stir until smooth.

• Heat the oil in a pan over high heat. Add the garlic and ginger and stir-fry about 1 minute. Add all the mushrooms, soy sauce, sugar, salt, and broth. Let the soup boil for about 10 minutes. Stir in the cornmeal mixture, and let the soup come to a boil again. Before serving, sprinkle with cilantro and grind some pepper over top.

Makes 6 servings.

PER SERVING:	152 CALORIES	
NUTRITIONAL INFORMATION		
Carbohydrate	19	g
Protein	8	g
Total fat	7	g
Cholesterol	0	mg
Sodium	2224	mg
Fiber	3	g

Hot-Sour Soup

From China • Classic

• Soak the shiitake mushrooms in warm water for about 20 minutes. Rinse the tofu under cold running water. Cut the tofu and bamboo shoots into sticks about 2 inches (4 cm) long.

• Drain shiitake mushrooms, then cut into thin strips. Trim the chile, wash, halve lengthwise, and cut into 1/2- to 1-inch- (2- to 3-cm)- long sticks. Wash and finely chop the chives. Wash cilantro and remove the roots; finely chop stems and leaves. Combine cornstarch with 2 tablespoons cold water and stir until smooth.

• Heat the vegetable broth in a large pot over medium heat. Add tofu, bamboo shoots, mushrooms, and chile, and let cook over low heat for about 3 minutes.

• Stir in soy sauce, salt, black pepper, sugar, su, and the cornstarch mixture. Let the soup come to a boil, then add sesame oil, sambal oelek, chives, and cilantro.

Makes 6 servings.

PER SERVING:	120 CALORIES	
NUTRITIONAL INFORMATION		
Carbohydrate	18	g
Protein	7	g
Total fat	4	g
Cholesterol	0	mg
Sodium	1231	mg
Fiber	2	g

Soup of Mixed Mushrooms

10 dried shiitake mushrooms*
about 1 lb (400 g) oyster mushrooms
2/3 lb (300 g) button mushrooms
2 (2-inch) pieces fresh ginger*
4 garlic cloves
2 bunches cilantro*
2 tablespoons cornmeal
2 tablespoons oil
scant 1/4 cup (45 ml) light soy sauce*
1 tablespoon brown sugar
1/2 teaspoon salt
1 1/2 quarts (1 1/2 l) vegetable broth (see page 9)
freshly ground black pepper

Preparation time: about 30 minutes

Hot-Sour Soup

6 medium size shiitake mushrooms*
1/3 lb (150 g) firm tofu
1/4 lb (100 g) bamboo shoots
1 hot red chile
1 bunch chives
1 bunch cilantro*
2 tablespoons cornstarch
1 quart plus 1 cup (1 1/4 l) vegetable broth (see page 9)
2 tablespoons light soy sauce*
salt
1/2 teaspoon freshly ground black pepper
3 tablespoons sugar
1/2 cup plus 2 tablespoons (150 ml) su*
1 teaspoon sesame oil*
1 tablespoon sambal oelek (see page 27)

Preparation time: about 35 minutes

Miso Soup

1 green onion
1/3 lb (150 g) silky tofu
1 1/2 quarts (1 1/2 l) vegetable broth (see page 9)
about 1/2 lb (200 g) red miso*

Preparation time:
about 15 minutes

Broth with Omelet Strips

2 bunches cilantro*
1 bunch chives
5 garlic cloves
5 eggs
generous 1/4 cup (75 ml) light soy sauce*, divided
scant 1/2 cup (100 ml) vegetable oil, divided
1 1/2 quarts (1 1/2 l) vegetable broth (see page 9)
1 teaspoon salt
freshly ground black pepper

Preparation time:
about 25 minutes

Miso Soup
From Japan • Pictured

• Trim and wash the green onion then cut into thin slices, including the green top.

• Cut the tofu into 1/2-inch- (1-cm)- thick slices.

• Combine vegetable broth and red miso in a pot and heat, stirring constantly with a whisk, until almost boiling. The soup should thicken slightly. Carefully place the tofu in the soup and let steep for about 1 minute.

• Divide the soup among 6 small bowls and garnish with green onion slices.

Makes 6 servings.

Broth with Omelet Strips
From Thailand • Mild

• Wash the cilantro and chives. Remove cilantro roots, then finely chop leaves and stems; chop chives. Peel and finely chop garlic. Whisk the eggs with 2 tablespoons soy sauce in a small bowl.

• Heat 5 tablespoons oil in a large frying pan. Add egg mixture, and cook about 1 minute; turn eggs and cook 1 more minute. Remove omelet from pan and let drain on paper towel.

• Heat remaining oil in the pan. Add garlic and stir-fry until golden, then set aside.

• Bring the vegetable broth to a boil in a pot. Cut the omelet into strips about 1/8 inch (1/2 cm) wide and 2 inches long; add omelet strips to the broth, and let boil for about 1 minute.

• Season the soup to taste with the remaining soy sauce and salt; sprinkle cilantro, chives, garlic, and black pepper over top.

Makes 6 servings.

PER SERVING:	164 CALORIES	
NUTRITIONAL INFORMATION		
Carbohydrate	18	g
Protein	11	g
Total fat	5	g
Cholesterol	0	mg
Sodium	3828	mg
Fiber	0	g

PER SERVING:	283 CALORIES	
NUTRITIONAL INFORMATION		
Carbohydrate	10	g
Protein	13	g
Total fat	23	g
Cholesterol	177	mg
Sodium	1839	mg
Fiber	0	g

Japanese Noodle Soup

1/3 lb (150 g) young carrots
about 1/4 lb (100 g) spinach
1 green onion
about 1 lb (400 g) udon noodles*
1 quart (1 l) vegetable broth (see page 9)
1 tablespoon sugar
1/2 teaspoon salt
1/4 cup (60 ml) Japanese soy sauce*
scant 1/4 cup (45 ml) mirin*

*Preparation time:
about 25 minutes*

Cellophane Noodle Soup

10 medium-size dried mu-err mushrooms*
about 1/4 lb (100 g) cellophane noodles
about 1 lb (400 g) spinach
5 garlic cloves
scant 1/4 cup (45 ml) vegetable oil
1 1/2 quarts (1 1/2 l) vegetable broth (see page 9)
scant 1/4 cup (45 ml) light soy sauce*
1/2 teaspoon salt
1 teaspoon sugar
freshly ground black pepper

*Preparation time:
about 25 minutes*

18

Japanese Noodle Soup
Easy to prepare

• Bring a large pot of water to a boil. Peel and trim the carrots, then cut into match sticks. Add carrot sticks to the boiling water and cook about 5 minutes; remove with a skimmer, and set aside. Pick over the spinach and wash in several changes of cold water. Add spinach to hard-boiling water and blanch for about 1 minute; drain in a colander. Trim the green onion, wash and cut into thin slices.

• Cook the noodles in the boiling water according to the directions on the package, taking care not to overcook; drain, rinse with cold water, and keep warm.

• Bring the vegetable broth to a boil in a large pot. Stir in sugar, salt, soy sauce, and mirin. Add the carrots and spinach to the broth, and stir until hot throughout. Distribute the noodles among 5 soup bowls, then fill with the hot broth. Garnish with green onion slices.

Makes 5 servings.

PER SERVING:	170 CALORIES	
NUTRITIONAL INFORMATION		
Carbohydrate	34	g
Protein	7	g
Total fat	2	g
Cholesterol	22	mg
Sodium	1901	mg
Fiber	2	g

Cellophane Noodle Soup
From Thailand • Pictured

• Soak the mu-err mushrooms in warm water for about 20 minutes.

• Meanwhile, soften the cellophane noodles in warm water for about 5 minutes. Pick over the spinach, and wash in several changes of cold water; halve large leaves. Drain the noodles in a colander, then cut into large pieces with kitchen scissors.

• Peel and finely chop the garlic. Heat the oil in a frying pan over medium-high heat. Add garlic and stir-fry until golden-brown; set aside.

• Drain the mushrooms in a colander. Remove any tough spots from the mushrooms, then cut them into bite-size pieces. Bring the vegetable broth to a boil in a large pot. Add the mushrooms, noodles, spinach, soy sauce, salt, and sugar. Let cook for about 1 minute. Stir in the garlic and grind pepper over top.

Makes 5 servings.

PER SERVING:	257 CALORIES	
NUTRITIONAL INFORMATION		
Carbohydrate	35	g
Protein	7	g
Total fat	13	g
Cholesterol	0	mg
Sodium	2331	mg
Fiber	3	g

Won Ton Soup

20 frozen won ton wrappers
(available at Asian grocery
stores and some supermarkets)
about $^1/_8$ lb (70 g) firm tofu
1 small carrot
about $^1/_8$ lb (50 g) water
chestnuts
1 oz (30 g) Szechuan
vegetables* (canned)
$^1/_2$ teaspoon sugar
1 teaspoon cornstarch
1 teaspoon salt, divided
scant $^1/_4$ cup (45 ml)
vegetable oil
about $^1/_4$ lb (100 g) spinach
$1^1/_2$ quarts ($1^1/_2$ l) vegetable
broth (see page 9)
freshly ground back pepper
sesame oil

Preparation time:
about 45 minutes

Spinach Soup

$1^1/_3$ lb (600 g) spinach
1 (12-oz/340-g) can whole-
kernel corn
5 shallots
3 (2-inch) pieces fresh ginger*
scant $^1/_4$ cup (45 ml)
vegetable oil
$1^2/_3$ cups (400 ml) coconut
milk
1 teaspoon sambal oelek
(see page 27)
$1^1/_2$ teaspoon salt
freshly grated nutmeg

Preparation time:
about 25 minutes

Won Ton Soup
From China • Pictured

• Let the won ton dough thaw out at room temperature.

• Rinse the tofu under running water. Peel the carrot. Rinse the water chestnuts. Cut tofu, carrot, water chestnuts, and Szechuan vegetables into small cubes. In a large bowl, combine sugar, cornstarch, $^1/_2$ teaspoon salt, and oil. Add diced vegetables and mix carefully.

• Place 1 teaspoon vegetable mixture in the center of each won ton wrapper. Fold the four corners of each wrapper over the filling and press together lightly in the middle to seal edges.

• Pick over the spinach, and wash in several changes of cold water; let drain, then chop coarsely. Bring the vegetable broth to a boil in a large pot; reduce heat. Carefully place the won ton dumplings in the hot broth, and let cook over low heat for about 3 minutes. Add the spinach, the remaining salt, pepper, and sesame oil.

Makes 5 servings.

Spinach Soup
From Indonesia • Easy to prepare

• Pick over the spinach and wash in several changes of cold water; let drain, then chop coarsely. Drain the corn. Peel and finely chop the shallots and ginger.

• Heat the oil in a large pot. Add shallots and ginger, and stir-fry about 1 minute. Add the spinach and the corn, cook until the spinach has wilted.

• Add the coconut milk, $^1/_2$ cup ($^1/_8$ l) water, sambal oelek, salt, and nutmeg. Let simmer for about 3 minutes.

Makes 5 servings.

Variations

Instead of coconut milk and water, you can use 3 cups ($^3/_4$ l) vegetable broth, seasoned with a little sesame oil. The soup will not be as creamy.

PER SERVING:	288 CALORIES	
NUTRITIONAL INFORMATION		
Carbohydrate	27	g
Protein	8	g
Total fat	18	g
Cholesterol	3	mg
Sodium	1858	mg
Fiber	1	g

PER SERVING:	363 CALORIES	
NUTRITIONAL INFORMATION		
Carbohydrate	18	g
Protein	7	g
Total fat	32	g
Cholesterol	0	mg
Sodium	941	mg
Fiber	7	g

Cucumber Soup with Lily Petals

From China • Pictured

• Soften the lily petals in warm water for about 20 minutes.

• Meanwhile, peel the cucumber, halve lengthwise, and scrape out the seeds. Cut cucumber halves into $1/8$-inch- ($1/2$-cm)- thick slices. Wash the tomatoes; quarter them, and remove the stems. Wash and finely chop the chives.

• Bring the vegetable broth to a boil in a large pot. Drain lily petals, then remove any hard ends. Add lily petals to broth; the petals can be added individually or knotted together. Add cucumber slices, and let simmer over low heat for about 10 minutes.

• Add the tomatoes, soy sauce, and salt, and let cook for about 3 minutes. Stir in sesame oil, then sprinkle the soup with chives and pepper.

Makes 6 servings.

Sour Vegetable Soup

From Indonesia • More time-consuming

• Soften the tamarind in warm water for about 20 minutes. Wash and trim the eggplant and zucchini; dice small, and place in a shallow casserole dish. Sprinkle with salt, and let drain for about 20 minutes. Wash the cabbage and cut into strips. Wash the beans, trim, and cut into pieces. Peel the shallots. Wash the chilies and remove stems. Chop shallots and chilies and mash in a mortar with the kemiri nuts.

• In a large pot, combine 1 cup ($1/4$ l) water, the shallot-chili paste and peanuts; bring to a boil, and boil about 3 minutes. Add laos, sugar, Indian bay leaves, cabbage, and beans; let simmer 5 more minutes.

• Press out the tamarind, reserving the juice and discarding the solids. Rinse the eggplant and zucchini; add to the soup with tamarind juice and salt to taste; let cook 10 more minutes.

Makes 6 servings.

Cucumber Soup with Lily Petals

$3/4$ oz (20 g) dried lily petals*
1 large cucumber
3 small tomatoes
1 bunch chives
1 quart plus 1 cup ($1^1/4$ l) vegetable broth (see page 9)
2 tablespoons light soy sauce*
1 teaspoon salt
1 teaspoon sesame oil*
freshly ground black pepper

Preparation time: about 30 minutes

Sour Vegetable Soup

4 (walnut-size) pieces pressed tamarind*
1 small eggplant
3 medium-size zucchini
$1^1/2$ teaspoons salt
about $1/2$ lb (200 g) cabbage (weighed after trimming)
about $1/2$ lb (200 g) long green beans*
5 shallots
2 red chilies
5 kemiri nuts
$1/4$ cup (50 g) roasted peanuts
1 pinch laos*
2 teaspoons sugar
2 Indian bay leaves* (salam)
1 quart (1 l) vegetable broth (see page 9)

Preparation time: about 30 minutes

PER SERVING:	41 CALORIES	
NUTRITIONAL INFORMATION		
Carbohydrate	6	g
Protein	3	g
Total fat	2	g
Cholesterol	0	mg
Sodium	1568	mg
Fiber	1	g

PER SERVING:	117 CALORIES	
NUTRITIONAL INFORMATION		
Carbohydrate	17	g
Protein	6	g
Total fat	5	g
Cholesterol	0	mg
Sodium	794	mg
Fiber	4	g

THE
JOY
OF...

Vegetables

Enormous Choice

The vegetable markets in Asia provide overwhelming proof of the vast array of vegetables available in this part of the world. In Bangkok, Jakarta, Ho-Chi-Minh City (formerly known as Saigon), Shanghai, and Tokyo, the choice is enormous.

If you ever have the opportunity to experience a bustling marketplace in any of these cities, you should take it—even if you have no intention of buying anything. You will find many familiar vegetables that thrive as well there as they do here, perhaps differing only in size, for example, cabbages, carrots, and tomatoes imported into Indonesia by the Dutch. Beyond the familiar, however, there are quite a few other vegetables that would be rewarding to try. The aromas from one of the many small cookshops might even entice you to eat a small, delicious vegetable dish right on the spot.

Floating Markets

A characteristic feature in Asia are the floating vegetable markets, such as the ones in Thailand, Bangkok, and in the Mekong Delta in Vietnam. The traders move from house to house in long, narrow, wooden boats, in which the vegetables are piled in baskets, or they stop for a while at certain spots in the city. The boats contain a gaily colored selection: chilies in different shades of red and green; light and dark lilies; peppers in green, red, orange, and yellow; pale-green garlic; green and red peppercorns; garlic chives; yellow bamboo shoots; white soybean sprouts; and more.

Stir-Frying

In Asia, vegetables most commonly are prepared in a frying pan or wok. To stir-fry, a little oil is placed in the pan and brought to high heat. Then the prepared vegetables, usually cut into bite-size pieces, are added, and are fried in the hot oil while being stirred and tossed constantly. Broth, soy sauce, or rice vinegar is used to deglaze the pan. This cooking method has several advantages. The cooking time is very brief, so valuable vitamins and minerals are retained, as is the fresh appearance of the vegetables. You also can enjoy the meal without having to stand over a hot stove for a long time.

The vegetables can be served separately, according to kind, or can be combined in delicious ways. When combinations are made, it is not only the flavor of the individual varieties that is taken into consideration, but also their texture and color. A hot sauce also goes well with many vegetable dishes. You will find the recipe for sambal oelek and for a simple chili sauce at the right side of this page. Of course, rice is always served with vegetable dishes.

Selection

You will find many Asian vegetable varieties in local Asian groceries and some of the larger supermarkets—and, fortunately, the choice is getting better all the time. Chinese cabbage and bean sprouts have won a solid position in the vegetable hierarchy here. Chinese radish, or daikon, which is an important vegetable in Chinese cuisine, also is found here.

Talk with the produce manager about the selection of Asian vegetables that is available, and ask him when is the best time to find them. Perhaps he can order particular varieties that he has not carried before, but that his wholesaler supplies. You will discover that a wide range of vegetables is available for your Asian vegetarian cuisine, allowing you to discover entirely new taste experiences.

Sambal Oelek—Hot Sauce from Indonesia

This fiery red sauce is quickly prepared and is really "hot": For about 1/2 cup, wash 20 red chilies; remove stems, and chop. Crush chilies in a mortar with some salt. Stir the paste in a frying pan over medium heat with about 1/2 cup oil; heat the mixture for about 10 minutes. Stir occasionally while mixture is cooking.

Simple Chili Sauce

This hot condiment from Thailand can be made very quickly: Crush 2 peeled garlic cloves in a mortar. Add 1/4 cup light soy sauce, 2 tablespoons lime juice and 1 tablespoon each of palm sugar and chili powder. Stir all until the sugar has dissolved.

27

scant $1/4$ lb (100 g) cellophane
noodles*
scant $1/2$ lb (200 g) broccoli
2 medium-size carrots
scant $1/2$ lb (200 g) Chinese
cabbage
scant $1/2$ lb (200 g) firm tofu
3 garlic cloves
scant $1/2$ cup (100 ml)
vegetable oil
scant $1/4$ cup (45 ml) light soy
sauce*
2 tablespoons dark soy sauce*
2 tablespoons sugar
$1/2$ teaspoon salt

Preparation time:
about 30 minutes

Fried Soybean Sprouts

3 (2-inch) pieces fresh ginger*
scant 1 lb (400 g) soybean
sprouts
1 bunch chives
5 garlic cloves
generous $1/4$ cup (75 ml)
vegetable oil
generous $1/4$ cup (75 ml) light
soy sauce*
$1/2$ teaspoon salt
1 tablespoon sugar

Preparation time:
about 20 minutes
(+ 20 minutes resting time)

28

Vegetables with Cellophane Noodles
From Thailand • Easy to prepare

• Soak the cellophane noodles in warm water for about 5 minutes, let drain, and coarsely chop. Wash and trim the broccoli, then cut it into small florets. Cut the stems into bite-size pieces. Peel and slice the carrots. Trim the Chinese cabbage and remove the individual leaves; wash, let drain, then coarsely chop.

• Cut the tofu into 2-inch- (5-cm)- long strips. Peel and mince the garlic. Heat the oil very hot in a frying pan. Add tofu and stir-fry for about 5 minutes, or until golden brown; remove tofu from oil and set aside. Add garlic to the pan, and stir-fry until golden-brown. Add the broccoli and carrots, and stir-fry over high heat, stirring constantly, for about 1 minute. Add the cellophane noodles, Chinese cabbage, soy sauces, and sugar, and stir-fry for about 1 minute. Stir in the tofu, then season with salt.

Makes 4 servings.

Fried Soybean Sprouts
From Vietnam • Pictured

• Peel the ginger and cut it into thin slices; cut the slices into sticks. Put the ginger in a bowl, cover with cold water, and let stand for 20 minutes.

• Meanwhile, wash the soybean sprouts and let them drain. Wash the chives and cut them into $1\frac{1}{2}$-inch- (4-cm)- long pieces. Peel and finely chop the garlic.

• Drain the ginger in a colander. Heat the oil in a frying pan over high heat. Add the garlic and stir-fry until golden-brown, being careful not to burn. Add ginger, soybean sprouts, soy sauce, salt, sugar, and chives. Stir-fry for about 1 minute. Correct the seasonings with sugar and soy sauce.

Makes 4 servings.

PER SERVING:	507 CALORIES	
NUTRITIONAL INFORMATION		
Carbohydrate	44	g
Protein	14	g
Total fat	33	g
Cholesterol	0	mg
Sodium	1883	mg
Fiber	5	g

PER SERVING:	317 CALORIES	
NUTRITIONAL INFORMATION		
Carbohydrate	22	g
Protein	19	g
Total fat	21	g
Cholesterol	0	mg
Sodium	4423	mg
Fiber	0	g

Banana Flowers in Coconut Milk

From Indonesia • Easy to prepare

• Drain the banana flowers; remove any tough parts. Cut the flowers into bite-size pieces. Peel and finely chop the shallots.

• Let the coconut milk come to a boil in a pot. Add the shallots, salt, and pepper, and simmer over low heat for about 1 minute.

• Add the banana flowers, and simmer for about 10 minutes, stirring often.

Sambal oelek tastes good with this (see page 27).

Makes 4 servings.

Spinach with Sesame

From Japan • Pictured

• Toast the sesame seeds in a dry frying pan, covered, for about 2 minutes; shake the pan constantly while the seeds are cooking so they don't burn. Place the seeds in a suribachi and mash with a pestle.

• Combine mashed sesame seeds in a dish with the sugar, soy sauce, and mirin.

• Bring a large pot of water to a boil. Pick over the spinach and wash it in several changes of cold water. Add spinach to boiling water and blanch about 1 minute. Drain the spinach in a colander, and carefully press out any excess water. Chop the leaves coarsely.

• Place the spinach in a serving dish and add the sauce; toss to coat the spinach, then season to taste.

Makes 4 servings.

Banana Flowers in Coconut Milk

2 ($17^2/_3$-oz/500-g) cans banana flowers
6 shallots
$1^2/_3$ cups (400 ml) coconut milk
1 teaspoon salt
freshly ground black pepper

Preparation time: about 20 minutes

Spinach with Sesame

$^1/_4$ cup (60 ml) light sesame seeds*
2 tablespoons sugar
$^1/_4$ cup (60 ml) Japanese soy sauce*
2 tablespoons mirin*
salt
$1^3/_4$ lb (800 g) spinach

Preparation time: about 25 minutes

PER SERVING:	230 CALORIES	
NUTRITIONAL INFORMATION		
Carbohydrate	6	g
Protein	2	g
Total fat	24	g
Cholesterol	0	mg
Sodium	596	mg
Fiber	2	g

PER SERVING:	148 CALORIES	
NUTRITIONAL INFORMATION		
Carbohydrate	18	g
Protein	9	g
Total fat	6	g
Cholesterol	0	mg
Sodium	1286	mg
Fiber	7	g

Stewed Black Salsify

From Japan • Pictured

• Put the shiitake mushrooms in a dish and cover with warm water; let soften for about 20 minutes.

• Meanwhile, clean and peel the carrots, then cut into thin 2-inch- (5-cm)- long sticks. Scrub the salsify with a brush; peel and cut into sticks the same size as the carrots. Wash the ginger and, without peeling, grate into a small bowl. Drain the mushrooms in a colander and press out excess water. Remove the stems, and cut the caps into small strips.

• Heat the oil in a wok over high heat. Add the carrots, salsify, and shiitake mushrooms and reduce heat to medium. Press out the ginger and stir the juice into the wok, along with the mirin, sugar, soy sauce, and pepper. Let stew, covered over low heat, with lid slightly ajar, for about 20 minutes.

Makes 4 servings.

Oyster Mushrooms with Basil

From Thailand • Easy to prepare

• Wash the oyster mushrooms, remove the hard base of the stems, and chop coarsely. Peel and finely chop the garlic. Wash the peppers, removing the stems, and chop fine. Mash the garlic and peppers into a paste with ¹/₂ teaspoon of salt in a mortar. Remove leaves from basil, discard stems, and wash.

• Heat the oil in a frying pan over high heat. Stir the paste into the oil, and stir-fry for about 1 minute. Add the mushrooms, soy sauce, sugar, about ¹/₄ cup (74 ml) water, and the remaining salt. Stir-fry over high heat for about 1 minute.

• Remove the pan from the stove, mix in the basil leaves and serve.

Makes 4 servings.

Stewed Black Salsify

5 medium-size shiitake mushrooms*
²/₃ lb (300 g) carrots
1¹/₄ lb (600 g) black salsify*
2 (2-inch) pieces fresh ginger*
¹/₄ cup (60 ml) vegetable oil
¹/₄ cup (60 ml) mirin*
2 tablespoons sugar
scant ¹/₄ cup (45 ml) Japanese soy sauce*
freshly ground black pepper

Preparation time: about 45 minutes

Oyster Mushrooms with Basil

1¹/₈ lb (500 g) oyster mushrooms
7 garlic cloves
2 hot red peppers
1 teaspoon salt
scant ¹/₄ lb (100 g) fresh red Thai basil* (bai grapau; Asian groceries)
generous ¹/₄ cup (74 ml) vegetable oil
scant ¹/₄ cup (45 ml) light soy sauce*
1¹/₂ teaspoons sugar

Preparation time: about 20 minutes

PER SERVING:	336 CALORIES	
NUTRITIONAL INFORMATION		
Carbohydrate	50	g
Protein	6	g
Total fat	14	g
Cholesterol	0	mg
Sodium	1421	mg
Fiber	7	g

PER SERVING:	204 CALORIES	
NUTRITIONAL INFORMATION		
Carbohydrate	12	g
Protein	7	g
Total fat	15	g
Cholesterol	0	mg
Sodium	1626	mg
Fiber	3	g

Corn in Banana Leaves

2 (12-oz/340-g) cans whole-kernel corn
2 stalks lemongrass*
*1 (1¹/₂-inch- /4-cm- long)
piece galangal**
2 (2-inch) pieces turmeric*
5 lemon leaves*
1 teaspoon salt
generous ¹/₄ cup (36 g) grated coconut
scant ¹/₄ cup (45 ml) light soy sauce*
2 tablespoons palm sugar*
generous ³/₄ cup (200 ml) coconut milk
1¹/₈ lb (500 g) banana leaves
Also:
toothpicks

*Preparation time:
about 55 minutes*

Corn in Banana Leaves
From Vietnam • More time-consuming

• Drain the corn in a colander. Wash the lemongrass and cut into thin slices. Peel and finely chop the galangal and turmeric. Wash the lemon leaves and let drain; roll lengthwise, then slice very thin.

• Mash the lemongrass, galangal, turmeric, and salt in a mortar. Add the grated coconut, and pound all ingredients to form a paste.

• In a large bowl, carefully combine the paste, corn kernels, soy sauce, palm sugar, and coconut milk; set aside.

• Carefully wipe the banana leaves with a damp cloth. Cut the leaves into 8-inch-(20-cm)- wide pieces. Lay two pieces together, overlapping them, and place 3 tablespoons of the corn mixture in the center of each pair of leaves.

• Fold the broad sides of the leaves over so that the edges have an overlap of ¹/₂ to 1 inch (2 to 3 cm). Fasten the leaves together with toothpicks. Fold both narrow sides toward the inside and also fasten with toothpicks.

• Lay the filled banana leaves on the grill. Grill about 3 minutes on each side. The outer banana leaves may become black.

Makes 4 servings.

Tip

Banana leaves can be found in Asian grocery stores. If you can't find them, you can substitute with doubled aluminum foil, but the taste and fragrance will not be the same.

PER SERVING:	792 CALORIES	
NUTRITIONAL INFORMATION		
Carbohydrate 140		g
Protein 18		g
Total fat 21		g
Cholesterol 0		mg
Sodium 1691		mg
Fiber 1		g

34

Sautéed Green Asparagus

about 1 1/2 lb (700 g) asparagus
2 teaspoons cornstarch
4 garlic cloves
3/8 cup (90 ml) vegetable oil
1 tablespoon sugar
2 tablespoons light soy sauce*
1/2 teaspoon salt
freshly ground black pepper
1 tablespoon sesame oil*

Preparation time:
about 20 minutes

Cauliflower with Chilies

4 garlic cloves
2 (2-inch) pieces fresh ginger*
2 red chilies
5 shallots
3 green onions
1 cauliflower (about 2 lbs/1 kg)
1 tablespoon plus 1/2 teaspoon salt
generous 1/4 cup (74 ml) vegetable oil
scant 1/4 cup (45 ml) soy sauce*
1 tablespoon sugar

Preparation time:
about 30 minutes

Sautéed Green Asparagus
From China • Perfect for company

• Bring about 2 quarts (2 l) water to a boil. Wash the asparagus. Cut off the tough ends. If necessary, peel the ends. Cut the asparagus into 2-inch- (5-cm)-long pieces. Blanch the asparagus in the boiling water for about 1 minute; pour in a sieve, rinse with cold water, and let drain.

• In a small bowl, combine cornstarch and 1 tablespoon cold water; stir until smooth. Peel and finely chop the garlic. Heat the oil in a frying pan or wok over high heat; add the garlic, and stir-fry until golden-brown. Add the asparagus and sauté, tossing constantly, over high heat for 1 minute. Add sugar, soy sauce, salt, pepper, and 1/2 cup plus 2 tablespoons water. Stir in the cornstarch. Drizzle the sesame oil over the asparagus.

Makes 5 servings.

Cauliflower with Chilies
From Indonesia • Pictured

• Peel and finely chop the garlic and ginger. Wash the chilies, remove and discard the stems, then cut chilies into thin sticks. Peel and finely chop the shallots. Trim and wash the green onions, then cut into 2-inch- (4-cm)-long pieces.

• Trim and wash the cauliflower; remove and discard the stalk, and cut the head into bite-size florets. Bring about 1 quart (1 l) water to a boil with 3 teaspoons salt. Add cauliflower and cook for about 5 minutes, then drain in a colander.

• Heat the oil in a frying pan over high heat. Add garlic, ginger, chilies, and shallots, and stir-fry for 2 minutes over high heat, stirring constantly. Add cauliflower, soy sauce, the remaining salt, sugar, and about 1/2 cup (1/8 l) water. Braise, covered, over medium heat for 10 minutes.

Makes 5 servings.

PER SERVING:	221 CALORIES	
NUTRITIONAL INFORMATION		
Carbohydrate	7	g
Protein	4	g
Total fat	20	g
Cholesterol	0	mg
Sodium	662	mg
Fiber	2	g

PER SERVING:	165 CALORIES	
NUTRITIONAL INFORMATION		
Carbohydrate	13	g
Protein	5	g
Total fat	12	g
Cholesterol	0	mg
Sodium	2480	mg
Fiber	6	g

Fried Daikon Radish with Egg
From Vietnam • Pictured

• Trim and peel the daikon radish, then cut into 1/8-inch- (1/2-cm)- thick sticks. Combine radish and su in a bowl; let marinate, covered, for about 1 hour.

• Meanwhile, peel and finely chop the garlic. Trim and wash the green onions, then halve them lengthwise, and slice into 1 1/2-inch- (4-cm)- long pieces.

• Drain the radish. Heat the oil very hot in a frying pan. Add garlic and stir-fry until golden-brown. Add the radish and green onions, then stir-fry for about 2 minutes. Stir in the soy sauce, salt, and sugar. Push the vegetables to the edges of the pan, leaving space in the center.

• Break the eggs into the space in the middle of the pan, stir, and let set. Divide the eggs into large sections, then mix the eggs with the vegetables. Fold in the chives.

Makes 5 servings.

Broccoli with Teriyaki Sauce
From China • Easy to prepare

• Trim and wash the broccoli, then cut into small florets. Cut off the stems and remove the lower, woody parts. Peel the stalk and cut into bite-size slices. Peel and finely chop the garlic. In a small bowl, combine the cornstarch with 2 tablespoons water and stir until smooth.

• In a large pot, bring the vegetable broth to a boil; add teriyaki sauce, 1/2 teaspoon salt, sugar, pepper, and sesame oil. Stir in the cornstarch and bring to a boil. Keep the sauce warm.

• Heat the oil in a frying pan or wok. Add the garlic and stir-fry until golden-brown. Add the broccoli and remaining salt, stir-fry over high heat for about 3 minutes. Arrange broccoli mixture on a plate and pour sauce over top.

Makes 5 servings.

Fried Daikon Radish with Egg

1 1/8 lb (500 g) daikon radish
1/2 cup (1/8 l) su*
5 garlic cloves
3 green onions
generous 1/4 cup (74 ml) vegetable oil
scant 1/4 cup (45 ml) light soy sauce*
1/2 teaspoon salt
1 tablespoon sugar
2 eggs
1 tablespoon chopped chives

Preparation time: about 15 minutes (+ 1 hour marinating time)

Broccoli with Teriyaki Sauce

1 1/4 lb (600 g) broccoli
4 garlic cloves
1 tablespoon cornstarch
1 cup (1/4 l) vegetable broth (see page 9)
generous 1/4 cup (74 ml) teriyaki sauce
1 1/2 teaspoons salt
1 tablespoon sugar
1/2 teaspoon freshly ground black pepper
1 teaspoon sesame oil*
3/8 cup (90 ml) vegetable oil

Preparation time: about 25 minutes

PER SERVING:	170 CALORIES	
NUTRITIONAL INFORMATION		
Carbohydrate	10	g
Protein	4	g
Total fat	13	g
Cholesterol	85	mg
Sodium	1106	mg
Fiber	2	g

PER SERVING:	215 CALORIES	
NUTRITIONAL INFORMATION		
Carbohydrate	13	g
Protein	5	g
Total fat	18	g
Cholesterol	0	mg
Sodium	1751	mg
Fiber	3	g

Vegetable Tempura

Vegetable Tempura

1 medium-size green bell pepper
¹/₄ lb (100 g) green asparagus
1 small eggplant
¹/₄ lb (100 g) broccoli
2 medium-size onions
¹/₄ lb (100 g) oyster mushrooms
¹/₄ lb (100 g) shiitake mushrooms*
2 egg yolks
1 cup flour
1 cup (100 g) cornmeal
salt
¹/₄ lb (100 g) daikon radish
2 (2-inch) pieces fresh ginger*
1 cup (¹/₄ l) vegetable broth (see page 9)
¹/₄ cup (60 ml) Japanese soy sauce*
¹/₄ cup (45 ml) mirin*
1 tablespoon sugar
1 quart (1 l) vegetable oil
flour for dusting

Preparation time: about 1 hour

Fried Eggplant

2 medium-size eggplants
salt
2 medium-size onions
2 red chilies
1 quart (1 l) vegetable oil
2 teaspoons Hungarian paprika
2 teaspoons brown sugar
¹/₄ cup (45 ml) light soy sauce*

Preparation time: about 25 minutes (+20 minutes resting time)

Vegetable Tempura
From Japan • Pictured

• Halve the bell pepper and remove seeds. Cut off the tough ends of the asparagus. Clean the eggplant and the broccoli. Peel the onions. Wash the vegetables and mushrooms, then let dry; cut into bite-size pieces.

• In a medium-size bowl, whisk the egg yolks with 1 cup (¹/₄ l) ice-cold water. In another bowl, mix flour, cornmeal, and salt, then carefully fold into the egg yolk mixture; set aside.

• For the sauce, clean and wash the daikon radish. Peel the ginger. Finely grate the radish and ginger, then combine in a large pot with the vegetable broth, soy sauce, mirin, and sugar; set aside.

• In a pot, heat the oil very hot. Dredge the vegetables and mushrooms in flour then dip each piece in the batter. Deep-fry battered vegetables in the oil for about 1 minute. Remove vegetables from the oil with a skimmer, and drain. Continue until all the vegetables are fried. Serve immediately with the sauce.

Makes 5 servings.

PER SERVING:	478 CALORIES	
NUTRITIONAL INFORMATION		
Carbohydrate	70	g
Protein	11	g
Total fat	18	g
Cholesterol	85	mg
Sodium	1118	mg
Fiber	8	g

Fried Eggplant
From Indonesia • Perfect for company

• Trim and wash the eggplant, then quarter lengthwise, and cut into ¹/₈-inch- (¹/₂-cm)- thick slices. Sprinkle with salt and drain for about 20 minutes.

• Meanwhile, peel the onions and cut into small dice. Wash the chilies, remove the stems, and chop fine.

• In a large pot, heat the oil very hot. Pat the eggplant slices dry. Place eggplant slices in the oil, and fry golden-brown, about 3 minutes. Lift eggplant out of the oil with a skimmer, and let drain on paper towels.

• Heat about ¹/₄ cup of the oil in a large frying pan over high heat; reserve the rest of the oil for another recipe. Add onions, chilies, paprika, sugar, and soy sauce to the frying pan, and stir to combine thoroughly. Add the eggplant to heat through.

Makes 5 servings.

PER SERVING:	250 CALORIES	
NUTRITIONAL INFORMATION		
Carbohydrate	13	g
Protein	2	g
Total fat	22	g
Cholesterol	0	mg
Sodium	886	mg
Fiber	3	g

NATUR
bEst
'S

Crisp Salads

Anyone whose knowledge of Asian cuisine comes mainly from the Chinese or Japanese restaurants around the corner, generally has no concept of the selection of salads available in those countries. The modest offering of raw prepared vegetables on the local Asian menu belies the wealth of vegetables produced in the region.

Feast for the Eye, Too

When salads are being prepared, consideration is given to ensuring that the individual ingredients not only complement each other in taste, but visually as well. The many shades of red and yellow chilies and peppers, tomatoes, and carrots beautifully contrast the sturdy green of the cucumber, green onions, and papayas.

As a rule, salads are not served in bowls but are presented on a large platter, better displaying the beauty of the arrangement.

Art to Eat

In Thailand, where the centuries-old tradition of fruit and vegetable cutting is brought to perfection, swans are crafted out of papayas, and complicated flowers out of carrots—decorations that really are a pity to eat. Instructions for two kinds of vegetable carvings, which are easy even for the novice, are on page 45.

Delicately Marinated

Most salads are made with a sweet-and-sour sauce, seasoned with a pinch of salt. The sour taste is derived by mild-flavored rice vinegar, su, the refreshing juice of limes, or the delicate tamarind juice.

Some salads are composed of blanched vegetables and are served lukewarm.

Rice also is eaten with the salads, which are served at the same time as other dishes of the meal.

Japan is the only Asian country in which a small dish of salad is served occasionally as an appetizer.

Healthy and Slimming

Asian salads are highly suitable for a dieter's buffet. Most of the salads are easy to prepare ahead of time because they rarely use delicate leaf lettuces, which can wilt after a short time. Firm ingredients like kohlrabi, soybean sprouts, carrots, radishes, cabbage, and sweet potatoes will hold well and still look fresh after sitting at room temperature for awhile. And in winter these vegetables are more healthful and flavorful than some greenhouse vegetables, which can be anemic in both taste and appearance, and can be loaded with pesticides.

The following choices would create a beautiful salad buffet:

Asparagus Salad from China (page 51)

Mixed Salad with Peanut Dressing from Indonesia (page 48)

Daikon Radish Salad from Japan (page 55)

Papaya Salad from Thailand (page 55)

Three-Vegetable Salad from Vietnam (page 47)

In addition, offer rice, grilled pepper strips, and whole button mushrooms to accompany the salads. Decorate the table in the appropriate style with suitable china—your guests will be enchanted!

For Cucumber Fans

Wash a cucumber and pat it dry. Halve it lengthwise, then cut off a 1-inch thick piece on the diagonal. Cut the piece crosswise, almost to the edge, into five to nine very thin, even slices. Be careful not to cut through to the edge. Leaving the first slice straight, carefully bend the second slice to the right to create a loop. Continue bending every other slice to create a fan effect. If your slices break when you bend them, they have been cut too thick; cut another 1-inch piece of cucumber on the diagonal and start over, making very thin slices.

Chili Flowers

Wash and dry the chili pepper. Remove the stem without cutting into the pepper. With a sharp knife, make several lengthwise cuts in the pepper down to the tip, leaving the stem end intact; remove the seeds. Trim the strips along the edges to form a point so that each strip looks like a flower petal. Place the pepper in cold water until ready to serve.

Tip

When working with chilies, be careful not to touch your eyes, and wash your hands thoroughly when you are through.

45

Three-Vegetable Salad

From Vietnam • Pictured

• Clean and peel carrots and daikon radish; cut each into ⅛-inch- (½-cm)- thick slices. Cut the slices into ⅛-inch- (½-cm)- thick match sticks. Place carrots and radish in a bowl. Add salt and toss to mix; let stand, covered, for about 45 minutes.

• Wash celery and cut into 2-inch- (4-cm)- long pieces.

• Rinse the carrots and radish sticks with cold water, then drain in a colander.

• Heat the oil in a frying pan over high heat. Add carrots, radish, celery, su, chili, sesame oil, sugar, and pepper; stir-fry for about 2 minutes; serve immediately.

Makes 6 servings.

Kohlrabi Salad

From China • Spicy

• In a large pot, bring 2 quarts (2 l) water and 1½ tablespoons salt to a boil. Meanwhile, peel the kohlrabi, removing any tough spots. Cut the kohlrabi into ⅛-by-2-inch (½-by-5-cm) match sticks. Add kohlrabi to boiling water and blanch for about 3 minutes. Drain in a colander and let cool.

• Peel and finely chop garlic and ginger. Wash the chilies and remove stems; finely chop. In a large bowl, thoroughly mix garlic, ginger, chilies, oil, sugar, su, remaining salt, and sesame oil. Combine the kohlrabi and sesame seeds in the bowl with the dressing; carefully toss to blend. Refrigerate the salad, covered, for at least 1 hour. Remove from refrigerator about 20 minutes before serving.

Makes 6 servings.

Three-Vegetable Salad

scant ½ lb (200 g) carrots
scant ½ lb (200 g) daikon radish
2 teaspoons salt
⅔ lb (300 g) cutting celery*
¼ cup (60 ml) vegetable oil
2 tablespoons su*
2 tablespoons chili oil*
1 tablespoon sesame oil*
2 teaspoons sugar
½ teaspoon freshly ground black pepper

Preparation time:
about 25 minutes
(+ 45 minutes resting time)

Kohlrabi Salad

2 tablespoons salt
2 lbs (1 kg) kohlrabi
3 garlic cloves
3 (2-inch) pieces fresh ginger*
3 red chilies
¼ cup (60 ml) vegetable oil
¼ cup (70 g) sugar
½ cup plus 2 tablespoons (150 ml) su*
1 tablespoon sesame oil*
2 tablespoons roasted sesame seeds*

Preparation time:
about 20 minutes
(+1 hour marinating time)

PER SERVING:	177 CALORIES
NUTRITIONAL INFORMATION	
Carbohydrate 9	g
Protein 1	g
Total fat 16	g
Cholesterol 0	mg
Sodium 841	mg
Fiber 3	g

PER SERVING:	201 CALORIES
NUTRITIONAL INFORMATION	
Carbohydrate 20	g
Protein 4	g
Total fat 13	g
Cholesterol 0	mg
Sodium 232	mg
Fiber 6	g

Mixed Salad with Peanut Dressing
From Indonesia • More time-consuming

For the salad:
scant ¹/₂ lb (200 g) trimmed
cabbage
2 medium-size carrots
1 large sweet potato (about
14 oz/400 g)
scant ¹/₂ lb (200 g) long green
beans or string beans*
2 teaspoons salt
scant ¹/₂ lb (200 g) soybean
sprouts
1 medium-size cucumber

For the dressing:
¹/₃ lb (150 g) roasted, salted
peanuts
3 garlic cloves
5 shallots
1 medium-size piece of
kencur*
scant ¹/₄ cup (45 ml) vegetable
oil
⁷/₈ cup (200 ml) coconut milk
2 tablespoons sugar
scant ¹/₄ cup (45 ml) fresh
lime juice
¹/₂ teaspoon chili powder

For garnish:
mint leaves

Preparation time:
about 1 hour

• Wash the cabbage leaves and cut into thin strips. Clean and peel the carrots; peel the sweet potato and cut both into thin strips. Wash and trim the beans; cut diagonally into 2-inch- (5-cm)- long pieces.

• Place the potato strips in a large pot and cover with warm salted water; bring to a boil. Cook about 10 minutes to parboil, then drain in a colander and let cool.

• Bring about 1 quart (1 l) water to a boil in a large pot. Add the beans, and let boil for about 2 minutes. Add the cabbage and carrots, and boil for about 2 minutes. Stir in the soybean sprouts, then pour all the vegetables into a colander and let drain.

• Peel the cucumber and halve lengthwise. Using a teaspoon, scrape out the seeds. Cut the cucumber halves into ¹/₈-inch- (¹/₂-cm)- thick slices.

• Mash the peanuts in the mortar, remove, and set aside. Peel the garlic and coarsely chop. Peel the shallots and cut into large cubes. In a mortar, combine the garlic and shallot pieces with 1 teaspoon salt; mash into a paste. Finely chop the kencur.

• Heat the oil in a frying pan over medium-high heat. Add the garlic-shallot paste and stir-fry until golden-brown, about 2 minutes. Add the peanuts, coconut milk, sugar, lime juice, chili powder, and kencur. Let all cook for about 2 minutes, stirring constantly. Remove the pan from the stove and let cool to lukewarm.

• Arrange the vegetables on a serving platter; pour the peanut dressing over top, then garnish with mint.

Makes 6 servings.

PER SERVING:	502 CALORIES	
NUTRITIONAL INFORMATION		
Carbohydrate .31		g
Protein 18		g
Total fat 39		g
Cholesterol 0		mg
Sodium 987		mg
Fiber 8		g

Asparagus Salad

From China • May be prepared in advance

• Bring about 2 quarts (2 l) water to a boil in a large pot. Wash the asparagus and cut off the tough ends. If necessary, peel the stalks 1 to 2 inches from the bottom, then cut into 2-inch- (5-cm)- long pieces. Add to boiling water and blanch for about 1 minute; drain in a colander under cold running water to stop the cooking.

• Peel the garlic and ginger; wash the chilies and remove the stems. Finely chop the garlic, ginger, and chilies.

• In a large bowl, combine garlic, ginger, chilies, lime juice, mirin, sugar, salt, soy sauce, vegetable oil, and sesame oil; stir until the sugar has dissolved. Add the asparagus and toss gently to coat. Marinate, covered, in the refrigerator for at least 2 hours. Remove from the refrigerator about 20 minutes before serving.

Makes 5 servings.

Vegetable-Fruit Salad

From Indonesia • Pictured

• Wash the chile, remove stem, and finely chop. In a large bowl, combine chile, lime juice, su, sugar, salt, and oil.

• Wash the Chinese cabbage leaves and cut into thin strips. Halve the pepper, remove the seeds and the white membranes; wash, then cut into $1/8$-inch- ($1/2$-cm)- wide strips. Peel the carrot and cut into very thin strips.

• Peel the oranges, removing all the white pith. With a sharp knife, cut the flesh out of the sections, and remove the seeds.

• Peel and quarter the apples, removing the seeds. Cut the quarters crosswise into thin slices. In a large salad bowl, combine the vegetables and fruit, then stir in the dressing, and toss to coat well.

Makes 5 servings.

Asparagus Salad

1³/4 lb (800 g) asparagus
5 garlic cloves
3 (2-inch) pieces fresh ginger*
3 red chilies
⁵/8 cup (150 ml) fresh lime juice
2 tablespoons mirin*
2 tablespoons sugar
1 teaspoon salt
generous ¹/4 cup (75 ml) light soy sauce*
generous ¹/4 cup (75 ml) vegetable oil
1 teaspoon sesame oil*

Preparation time: about 25 minutes (+ 2 hours marinating time)

Vegetable-Fruit Salad

1 red chile
¹/4 cup (60 ml) fresh lime juice
2 tablespoons su*
¹/4 cup (70 g) sugar
¹/2 teaspoon salt
2 tablespoons vegetable oil
1 small Chinese cabbage (about ¹/2 lb/200 g trimmed)
1 medium-size green bell pepper
1 large carrot
2 oranges
2 medium-size tart apples (such as Granny Smith)

Preparation time: about 25 minutes

PER SERVING:	208 CALORIES	
NUTRITIONAL INFORMATION		
Carbohydrate	22	g
Protein	5	g
Total fat	12	g
Cholesterol	0	mg
Sodium	1451	mg
Fiber	2	g

PER SERVING:	171 CALORIES	
NUTRITIONAL INFORMATION		
Carbohydrate	30	g
Protein	2	g
Total fat	6	g
Cholesterol	0	mg
Sodium	249	mg
Fiber	4	g

10 large dried shiitake
mushrooms*
10 large dried mu-err
mushrooms*
²/₃ lb (300 g) oyster
mushrooms
²/₃ lb (300 g) button
mushrooms
8 shallots
¹/₄ lb (100 g) fresh celery
greens
¹/₈ lb (50 g) mint leaves
5 red Thai chilies
¹/₄ cup (60 ml) fresh lime
juice
scant ¹/₄ cup (45 ml) light soy
sauce*
¹/₂ teaspoon salt
2 tablespoons sugar

Preparation time:
about 30 minutes

Mixed Mushroom Salad
From Thailand • Perfect for company

• Combine the shiitake and the mu-err mushrooms in a large bowl; cover with warm water and let soak for about 20 minutes.

• Meanwhile, wash the oyster mushrooms; trim the mushrooms, then tear them into large chunks. If necessary, wash the button mushrooms, trim and cut in half.

• Peel the shallots and cut them into thin slices. Wash the celery greens and coarsely chop. Wash the mint and shake it dry. Wash the chilies, remove the stems, then cut into thin slices.

• Drain the shiitake and mu-err mushrooms in a colander; cut out any hard spots, then cut mushrooms into bite-size pieces. Bring about 1 quart (1 l) water to a boil in a large pot. Add the mushrooms and blanch for about 1 minute; pour into a colander and let drain thoroughly. Let the mushrooms cool.

• Combine the shallots, celery greens, mint leaves, chilies, lime juice, soy sauce, salt, and sugar in a large bowl; stir and season to taste. The dressing should taste sweet, sour, and hot. Add the mushrooms to the dressing, and toss carefully to coat well. Serve the salad immediately.

Makes 5 servings.

Tip
The light soy sauce is especially popular in Thailand. Its flavor is not as intense as darker soy sauces, and it will not darken the color of the ingredients as much.

PER SERVING:	123 CALORIES
NUTRITIONAL INFORMATION	

Carbohydrate	25	g
Protein	6	g
Total fat	1	g
Cholesterol	0	mg
Sodium	971	mg
Fiber	4	g

Daikon Radish Salad

From Japan • Easy to prepare

• Peel and finely grate the horseradish and ginger. Cut the date into small cubes.

• Trim and peel the daikon radish, then coarsely grate. Place grated radish in a kitchen towel; squeeze the juice out and put gratings into a bowl.

• Add the su, sugar, and salt, and mix all well. Fold in the horseradish, ginger, and date. Taste and adjust the seasonings, then garnish with mint leaves.

Makes 4 servings.

PER SERVING:	59 CALORIES	
NUTRITIONAL INFORMATION		
Carbohydrate 12	g
Protein 1	g
Total fat 1	g
Cholesterol 2	mg
Sodium 116	mg
Fiber 2	g

Papaya Salad

From Thailand • Pictured

• Peel the papayas, then halve lengthwise; remove the black seeds with a spoon. Briefly rinse the papaya halves, then cut into thin slices; cut slices into thin strips.

• Peel the garlic. Wash the chilies and remove the stems. Wash the tomatoes, and cut them into eighths, removing the stems. Combine the garlic, chilies, and 1/2 teaspoon salt in a mortar and mash. Add the peanuts and mash coarsely. Stir in the palm sugar and mash into a paste.

• Place the paste in a large bowl, then add lime juice, soy sauce, and the remaining salt; mix well. Taste and adjust seasonings; the dressing should be sweet, sour, and sharp. Stir the papaya strips and tomato wedges into the dressing, and serve immediately.

Makes 4 servings.

Tip

If you mash the papaya strips a little, the salad becomes even juicier.

PER SERVING:	159 CALORIES	
NUTRITIONAL INFORMATION		
Carbohydrate 26	g
Protein 6	g
Total fat 4	g
Cholesterol 0	mg
Sodium 1658	mg
Fiber 3	g

Daikon Radish Salad

1 (2-inch) piece of horseradish, or
1 tablespoon prepared horseradish
1 (2-inch) piece of fresh ginger*
1 pitted date
1 (1 1/8 lb/500 g) daikon radish
1/4 cup (60 ml) su*
2 tablespoons sugar
salt

For garnish:
mint leaves

Preparation time:
about 20 minutes

Papaya Salad

2 medium-size, unripe Papayas (1 1/4 lb/600 g)
3 garlic cloves
4 red Thai chilies
3 medium-size tomatoes
1 teaspoon salt
3 to 4 tablespoons (50 g) roasted salted peanuts
2 tablespoons palm sugar*
1/4 cup (60 ml) fresh lime juice
scant 1/4 cup (45 ml) light soy sauce*

Preparation time:
about 25 minutes

Soybean Sprout Salad

1 1/8 lb (500 g) soybean sprouts
1 (2-inch) piece fresh ginger*
salt
2 eggs
2 tablespoons vegetable oil
1/4 cup (60 ml) su*
2 tablespoons mirin*
scant 1/4 cup (45 ml)
Japanese soy sauce*
1 teaspoon sesame oil*
2 tablespoons chopped
chives

Preparation time:
about 20 minutes
(+ 10 minutes resting time)

Salad with Fried Eggs

2 bunches cilantro*
2 medium-size onions
5 red Thai chilies
3 medium-size tomatoes
1/4 cup (60 ml) fresh lime
juice
2 tablespoons sugar
scant 1/4 cup (45 ml) light
soy sauce*
1 teaspoon salt
generous 1/4 cup (74 ml)
vegetable oil
5 eggs, lightly beaten

Preparation time:
about 30 minutes

Soybean Sprout Salad

From Japan • Refreshing

• Remove the ends from the soybean sprouts. Let the sprouts soak in cold water for about 10 minutes. Peel the ginger and cut into thin strips; let ginger strips soak in cold water for about 10 minutes.

• Bring a large pot of salted water to a boil. Drain the soybean sprouts, then add to boiling water and blanch for about 1 1/2 minutes. Drain and let cool.

• In a small bowl whisk the eggs with some salt. Heat the oil in a frying pan over medium-high heat. Add the eggs and swirl in the pan to make a thin omelet; cut into strips.

• In a large bowl, combine the su, mirin, soy sauce, and sesame oil. Add the soybean sprouts, the drained ginger, and the egg strips, and toss to coat with the dressing; garnish with chives.

Makes 4 servings.

PER SERVING:	295 CALORIES	
NUTRITIONAL INFORMATION		
Carbohydrate	20	g
Protein	21	g
Total fat	19	g
Cholesterol	106	mg
Sodium	1158	mg
Fiber	0	g

Salad with Fried Eggs

From Thailand • Pictured

• Wash the cilantro, remove the roots, then chop the stems and leaves. Peel the onions, halve lengthwise, then cut into thin slices. Wash the chilies, removing the stems, then finely chop. Wash the tomatoes; halve lengthwise, removing the stems, then cut into thick slices.

• In a large bowl, mix the chilies, lime juice, sugar, soy sauce, and salt.

• Heat the oil in a frying pan over medium heat. Add the eggs and cook for about 2 minutes. Drain the eggs on paper towels then cut into bite-size squares.

• Add the eggs, cilantro, onions, and tomatoes to the dressing, and toss to blend.

Makes 4 servings.

PER SERVING:	308 CALORIES	
NUTRITIONAL INFORMATION		
Carbohydrate	26	g
Protein	11	g
Total fat	20	g
Cholesterol	265	mg
Sodium	1123	mg
Fiber	3	g

Cucumber Salad with Tamarind Juice
From Thailand • Easy to prepare

• Place the tamarind in a bowl and cover with ¹/₂ cup warm water; let soften for about 20 minutes.

• Meanwhile, place the cellophane noodles in a bowl and cover with warm water; let soften about 5 minutes. Drain the cellophane noodles in a colander and cut into large pieces with kitchen scissors. Bring about 1 quart (1 l) water to a boil in a large pot. Add cellophane noodles and blanch for about 1 minute; drain in a colander and set aside.

• Peel the cucumber, halve it length-wise, and cut it into medium thin slices. Halve the tomatoes and remove the stems. Cut the halves into thin slices.

• Wash the celery greens, chives, and cilantro; cut each into 1-inch- (3-cm)-long pieces. Peel the onions, halve, and cut into thin slices. Wash the chilies, removing the stems, and finely chop. Coarsely mash the peanuts in a mortar.

• Knead the tamarind, and press it through a fine-mesh strainer reserving the juice. Combine 4 tablespoons tamarind juice in a large bowl with the soy sauce, salt, palm sugar, peanuts, and chilies. Taste and adjust the seasonings; the dressing should be sweet-sour-salty.

• Add cucumber and tomato slices, celery greens, chives, cilantro, onions, and cellophane noodles to the salad dressing. Taste and adjust seasonings again; serve immediately.

Makes 5 servings.

Tip
If you don't want it so hot, remove the seeds from the chilies. After handling chilies, wash your hands thoroughly before touching your face or other sensitive areas.

Cucumber Salad with Tamarind Juice

2 (walnut-size) pieces pressed tamarind*
¹/₈ lb (50 g) cellophane noodles*
1 medium-size cucumber
2 medium-size tomatoes
¹/₈ lb (50 g) celery greens
1 bunch chives
2 bunches cilantro*
2 medium-size onions
2 red Thai chilies
3 to 4 tablespoons (50 g) roasted salted peanuts
scant ¹/₄ cup (45 ml) light soy sauce*
1 teaspoon salt
2 tablespoons palm sugar*

Preparation time: about 40 minutes

PER SERVING:	152 CALORIES	
NUTRITIONAL INFORMATION		
Carbohydrate	27	g
Protein	4	g
Total fat	4	g
Cholesterol	0	mg
Sodium	1335	mg
Fiber	3	g

The **Mighty** Bean

Totally Tofu

Also known as soy bean curd or bean curd, tofu is the backbone, so to speak, of the vegetarian cuisine because it provides the protein that is crucial to the human body, but is not present in fruits and vegetables.

An Invention of Genius

Tofu was invented more than 2,000 years ago in China, when the Taoists were experimenting with a variety of healthy elixirs in search of eternal life. They got a bit nearer their goal with the somewhat accidental invention of bean curd. Tofu doesn't grant eternal life, but it might promote a longer one. In contrast to meat, tofu contains no cholesterol. Anyone who opts to eat soybean curd instead of meat is better protected against heart disease.

Originally called *dou fu*, tofu received its name in Japan, where it is part of the daily diet. Tofu has long played the role in Asian cuisine that is filled by meat in the Western world, and tofu dishes abound.

Numerous Varieties

Tofu is made from soybean milk and a curdling agent. The preparation is not simple, but is somewhat comparable to cheese production. The soybeans must first be dried for months; they are then softened with water, then pressed. Calcium sulfate is added to the resulting "milk," which starts the curdling process. In Japan, there are seven tofu varieties; in China, there are said to be 150. In the recipes in this book, only two varieties are used: firm and silky tofu.

Firm and Silky

In Asia, the firm varieties are most popular because they can be used in a wide variety of ways. Firm tofu can be stir-fried, boiled, deep-fried, and grilled, and it is used in many dishes, a well as for a garnish.

Silky tofu is soft and smooth, and melts in the mouth like yogurt or pudding. The texture is most comparable to flan. Silky tofu is eaten ice-cold in Japan during heat waves, sprinkled with freshly grated ginger and drizzled with soy sauce. This combination is refreshing and very popular. Thus, many manufacturers only produce silky tofu in the summer months, when the demand is the greatest.

True culinary talent is revealed when preparing tofu, for it demands sensitivity in seasoning the bland curd, and some creativity to lend it color and fragrance.

Be careful not to confuse the two kinds of tofu: Silky tofu is not suitable for deep-frying, grilling, or stir-frying, for it melts into a white broth. On the other hand, it tastes terrific added to soup.

Where You Get Tofu

Buy tofu as fresh as possible in Asian or health-food stores. Tofu also is available in most supermarkets. Be aware of the expiration date stamped on packaged tofu. If it isn't clearly visible, ask your grocer. Tofu stays fresh for seven to ten days. You can buy silky tofu in cake form in Asian stores. Instant silky tofu, for making at home, is available in some Asian stores. The instant tofu includes a packet of soybean powder and a lactone curdling agent.

Keeping Tofu

• Tofu should always be kept in the refrigerator. It can be kept frozen for about 3 months, but the texture will become chewier when thawed.

• To keep tofu fresh, rinse it, place it in a bowl of water, and store it, covered, in the refrigerator. Change the water daily; the tofu will stay fresh for up to 10 days.

• Before using tofu, always let it drain thoroughly.

2 (walnut-size) pieces pressed
tamarind*
$2/3$ lb (300 g) firm tofu
5 garlic cloves
7 shallots
7 large dried chilies
$1/3$ lb (150 g) oyster mushrooms
3 medium-size tomatoes
1 small head iceberg lettuce
2 medium-size carrots
1 cucumber
1 teaspoon salt
1 cup (237 ml) vegetable oil
$1/4$ cup (60 ml) light soy sauce*
2 tablespoons palm sugar*

*Preparation time:
about 35 minutes*

Vegetables with Tofu Dip

From Thailand • May be prepared in advance

• Place the tamarind in a bowl and cover with warm water; soften for about 20 minutes.

• Meanwhile, rinse the tofu under cold running water. Place tofu in a medium-size bowl, and mash it with a fork.

• Peel and mince the garlic and shallots.

• Place the chilies in a large bowl and cover with warm water; soak for about 10 minutes.

• Wash the oyster mushrooms, removing any hard spots, then finely chop. Wash the tomatoes, removing the stem, then coarsely dice.

• Pick over the lettuce, wash, and shake dry. Tear the head into large hunks. Clean and peel the carrots and cucumber. Slice the carrots and cucumber into $1/8$-inch- ($1/2$-cm)- thick slices. Arrange lettuce, carrots, and cucumber on a large platter.

• Knead the tamarind and press through a fine-meshed strainer, reserving the juice. Drain chilies. In a mortar, combine chilies and $1/2$ teaspoon salt; mash to a fine paste.

• In a frying pan, heat $5/8$ cup oil to very hot. Add the tofu and stir-fry about 5 minutes or until golden-brown. Remove tofu from the pan with a skimmer or slotted spoon. Heat the remaining oil in the pan, and add garlic and shallots; stir-fry until golden-brown.

• Add chili paste and tofu to the pan. Mix carefully and stir-fry about 1 minute. Add the oyster mushrooms, tomatoes, $1/4$ cup tamarind juice, soy sauce, the remaining salt, and palm sugar; let cook for about 5 minutes, or until all of the liquid has evaporated. Taste and adjust seasonings with tamarind juice, palm sugar, and salt. Serve with Basic Fragrant Rice (page 81).

Makes 4 servings.

PER SERVING:	632 CALORIES
NUTRITIONAL INFORMATION	

Carbohydrate 24	g
Protein 10	g
Total fat 58	g
Cholesterol 0	mg
Sodium 1667	mg
Fiber 4	g

Fried Tofu with Vegetables

From Thailand • Easy to prepare

• Rinse the tofu under cold running water, let drain, then cut into 2-by-1/2-inch- (4-by-1½-cm)- long pieces.

• Wash the broccoli, trim, and divide into small florets. Peel the stalk and cut into bite-size pieces.

• Discard the outer leaves of the Chinese cabbage. Remove and wash the remaining leaves; tear leaves into large pieces. Clean and peel the carrot; cut into thin slices. Peel the onions, halve them, then cut into 1/8-inch- (1/2-cm)- thick slices. Wash the soybean sprouts and let drain. Peel and finely chop the garlic.

• In a large frying pan, heat 5/8 cup oil to very hot. Add the tofu and stir-fry until golden-brown on all sides, about 5 minutes. Remove tofu pieces from the pan with a skimmer or slotted spoon.

• Heat remaining oil in the pan over high heat. Add the garlic and stir-fry until golden-brown. Add the broccoli, carrot, and onion. Stir-fry over high heat for about 1 minute.

• Add the Chinese cabbage, soybean sprouts, soy sauces, salt, and sugar; cook for another minute. In a small bowl, combine cornmeal with 1/4 cup water and stir until smooth. Add cornmeal mixture to the vegetables, and let come to a boil briefly. Add the tofu. Taste and adjust seasonings with soy sauce, salt, and sugar. Serve with a dish of chili powder on the side.

Makes 5 servings.

Variations

Use any combination of vegetables, depending on availability.

Fried Tofu with Vegetables
2/3 lb (330 g) firm tofu
1/4 lb (100 g) broccoli
1/4 lb (100 g) Chinese cabbage
1 large carrot
2 medium-size onions
1/3 lb (150 g) soybean sprouts
4 garlic cloves
3/4 cup (180 ml) vegetable oil
scant 1/4 cup (45 ml) light soy sauce*
1 tablespoon dark soy sauce*
1 teaspoon salt
2 tablespoons sugar
2 tablespoons cornmeal
chili powder

*Preparation time:
about 30 minutes*

PER SERVING:	498 CALORIES	
NUTRITIONAL INFORMATION		
Carbohydrate	24	g
Protein	17	g
Total fat	40	g
Cholesterol	0	mg
Sodium	1524	mg
Fiber	4	g

Crispy Tofu

7/8 lb (400 g) firm tofu
2 teaspoons salt
4 garlic cloves
1/2 bunch chives
1 tablespoon sesame oil*
1/4 cup (54 g) sugar
2 tablespoons su*
1/2 cup (120 ml) light soy sauce*
2 cups (1/2 l) vegetable oil
flour for dusting

Preparation time:
about 40 minutes

Fried Tofu with Cabbage

1 quart (1 l) vegetable oil
1/2 lb (200 g) firm tofu
7/8 lb (400 g) cabbage
1/3 lb (150 g) soybean sprouts
3 garlic cloves
2 tablespoons bean sauce*
2 tablespoons sugar
scant 1/4 cup (45 ml) light soy sauce*
2 tablespoons mirin*
1 tablespoon sesame oil*

Preparation time:
about 40 minutes

Crispy Tofu
From Japan • Mild

• Rinse the tofu under running cold water, then cut into strips about 2³/₄ inches (7 cm) long, 1¹/₂ inches (4 cm) wide, and ¹/₂ inch (1 cm) thick. Place the strips in a large bowl, sprinkle with salt, and cover with water. Let the tofu sit, covered, at room temperature for about 30 minutes.

• Meanwhile, peel and mince the garlic for the sauce. Wash the chives and cut into small pieces. In a large bowl, combine the sesame oil, sugar, su, and soy sauce and mix until sugar dissolves. Add the garlic and chives.

• Heat the oil in a high-sided frying pan or wok over high heat. Put some flour on a plate. Drain the tofu strips, then roll in the flour, and add to the very hot oil. Stir-fry the strips until golden-brown, about 3 minutes. Remove tofu from oil with a skimmer and let drain on paper towels. Serve the tofu with the sauce on the side.

Makes 5 servings.

PER SERVING:	441 CALORIES	
NUTRITIONAL INFORMATION		
Carbohydrate	27	g
Protein	16	g
Total fat	32	g
Cholesterol	0	mg
Sodium	2588	mg
Fiber	2	g

Fried Tofu with Cabbage
From China • Pictured

• In a large pot, heat 1 quart (1 l) oil until very hot. Meanwhile, rinse the tofu under cold running water, pat dry, then cut into strips about 2 inches (5 cm) long, ¹/₂ inch (2 cm) wide, and ¹/₈ inch (¹/₂ cm) thick. Add tofu to hot oil and stir-fry for about 3 minutes; remove tofu from pan with a skimmer, and let drain on paper towels. When cool enough to handle, set aside ¹/₂ cup oil and store the remaining oil for another use.

• Discard the outermost leaves of the cabbage. Quarter the cabbage, removing the stalk, then cut cabbage into bite-size pieces. Wash the soybean sprouts and let drain. Peel and finely chop the garlic.

• Heat the reserved ¹/₂ cup oil in a frying pan over high heat. Add the garlic and stir-fry until golden-brown. Add the cabbage, bean sauce, sugar, soy sauce, mirin, and sesame oil and fry for about 2 minutes over high heat. Add the soybean sprouts and tofu and fry long enough to heat through, about 1 minute.

Makes 5 servings.

PER SERVING:	381 CALORIES	
NUTRITIONAL INFORMATION		
Carbohydrate	19	g
Protein	14	g
Total fat	31	g
Cholesterol	0	mg
Sodium	1167	mg
Fiber	2	g

Tofu-Panang

From Thailand • Spicy

• Rinse the tofu under cold running water, let drain, then cut into pieces about 1½ inches (4 cm) long, ½ inch (2 cm) wide, and ⅛ inch (½ cm) thick. Wash and trim the button mushrooms, then cut them into halves. Wash the lemon leaves, shake dry, then cut them into very thin strips. Wash the pepper, remove the stem, and cut lengthwise into thin strips.

• Heat the oil very hot in a frying pan. Add the tofu and stir-fry until golden-brown; remove from the pan with a skimmer. Add curry paste to the pan and stir-fry about 1 minute.

• Set aside 3 tablespoons of the thick part of the coconut milk. Add the remaining coconut milk to the pan, along with soy sauce, palm sugar, salt, and lemon leaf strips; let simmer, stirring constantly, for about 2 minutes. Add the tofu, mushrooms, and pepper strips and let simmer 1 more minute. Taste and adjust seasonings with soy sauce and sugar. Garnish the dish with the 3 tablespoons of the reserved coconut milk.

Makes 5 servings.

PER SERVING:	515 CALORIES	
NUTRITIONAL INFORMATION		
Carbohydrate	19	g
Protein	15	g
Total fat	45	g
Cholesterol	0	mg
Sodium	1075	mg
Fiber	3	g

Tofu with Cashews

From China • Pictured

• In a large pot, heat 1 quart oil until very hot. Rinse the tofu under cold running water, pat dry, then cut into pieces about 1 inch (3 cm) long, ½ inch (1 cm) wide, and ⅛ inch (½ cm) thick. Add tofu to hot oil and fry until golden-brown, about 3 minutes; remove from oil with skimmer, and drain on paper towels. When oil is cool enough to handle, set aside ½ cup, and store remaining oil for another use.

• Peel and finely chop the garlic. Wash the chilies, removing the stems, then finely chop. In a small bowl, combine the bean sauce, sugar and chilies; mix well, mashing the beans.

• Heat the reserved ½ cup oil in a frying pan over high heat. Add the garlic and stir-fry until golden-brown. Stir in the bean-sauce mixture, soy sauce, mirin, ketchup, and enough water to reach desired sauce consistency. Add the tofu and cashews. Let simmer for about 4 minutes. Drizzle sesame oil over top before serving.

Makes 5 servings.

PER SERVING:	749 CALORIES	
NUTRITIONAL INFORMATION		
Carbohydrate	34	g
Protein	15	g
Total fat	65	g
Cholesterol	0	mg
Sodium	1279	mg
Fiber	2	g

Tofu-Panang

⅞ lb (400 g) firm tofu
½ lb (200 g) button mushrooms
5 lemon leaves*
1 hot red pepper
1⅔ cups (400 ml) coconut milk
⅝ cup (150 ml) vegetable oil
2 tablespoons Panäng curry paste*
¼ cup (60 ml) light soy sauce*
¼ cup (54 g) palm sugar*
½ teaspoon salt

Preparation time: about 20 minutes

Tofu with Cashews

1 quart (1 l) vegetable oil
⅞ lb (400 g) firm tofu
3 garlic cloves
3 red chilies*
¼ cup (60 ml) bean sauce*
scant ¼ cup (54 g) sugar
2 tablespoons light soy sauce*
2 tablespoons mirin*
2 tablespoons ketchup
1½ cups (250 g) roasted cashews
1 tablespoon sesame oil*

Preparation time: about 30 minutes

Green-Curry Tofu

$^7/_8$ lb (400 g) firm tofu
1 (19-oz/540-g) can bamboo shoots
$3^1/_2$ oz (100 g) green Thai basil leaves* (bai horapha)
5 lemon leaves* (kaffir lime leaves)
1 hot red pepper
$1^2/_3$ cups (400 ml) coconut milk
1 tablespoon hot green curry paste*
scant $^1/_4$ cup (45 ml) light soy sauce*
$^1/_2$ teaspoon salt
2 tablespoons palm sugar*

*Preparation time:
about 20 minutes*

Green-Curry Tofu
From Thailand . Spicy

• Rinse the tofu under cold running water, let drain, then cut into pieces about $1^1/_2$ inches (4 cm) long, $^1/_2$ inch ($1^1/_2$ cm) wide, and $^1/_4$ inch (1 cm) high. Rinse the bamboo shoots; halve them lengthwise, then slice thin.

• Wash the basil and lemon leaves, and shake dry. Roll the lemon leaves lengthwise and slice into very thin strips. Wash the hot pepper and remove the stem. Halve the pepper lengthwise, removing the seeds, and cut into thin strips.

• Take 3 tablespoons of the thick part of the coconut milk and bring to a boil in a large pan. Stir in the curry paste and let cook about 3 minutes over low heat, stirring constantly. Add the tofu pieces and lemon leaf strips, and let simmer for 1 minute more.

• Add the remaining coconut milk, 1 cup water, the bamboo shoot slices, soy sauce, salt, and palm sugar. Cook over low heat for about 3 minutes. Stir in the basil leaves and hot pepper strips. Taste and adjust seasonings with salt and palm sugar.

Makes 5 servings.

Tip
Green-Curry Tofu is a particularly hot dish. Add the hot green curry paste a little at a time, according to taste.

PER SERVING:	367 CALORIES	
NUTRITIONAL INFORMATION		
Carbohydrate 20	g
Protein 18	g
Total fat 27	g
Cholesterol 0	mg
Sodium 1101	mg
Fiber 4	g

Steamed Coconut Tofu

From Indonesia • Pictured

• Rinse the tofu under cold running water, cut into pieces, then place in a large bowl and mash with a fork. Peel and finely chop the shallots and garlic; finely chop the Indian bay leaves. Add garlic, shallots, and bay leaves to the tofu.

• Wash and finely chop the chives and cilantro. Set aside some cilantro for garnish. Wash the chilies, removing the stems, then finely chop.

• Add the chives, the remaining cilantro, chilies, sugar, lime juice, coconut milk, eggs, and salt to the bowl with tofu; mix well. Pour the mixture into an ovenproof bowl and place the bowl in a steamer; steam for 40 to 50 minutes.

• Toast the grated coconut in a dry pan until golden-brown. Turn the coconut tofu out onto a serving plate, and sprinkle with coconut and the remaining cilantro.

Makes 5 servings.

Tofu with Soybean Sprouts

From Vietnam • Easy to prepare

• Rinse the tofu under cold running water, then drain for several minutes. Cut the tofu into pencil-thick pieces about 2 inches (5 cm) long. Peel the carrot and cut into small match sticks. Rinse the soybean sprouts in cold water and drain. Trim and wash the green onions; cut into 2-inch- (5-cm-) long pieces.

• Heat the oil very hot in a large pot. Add the tofu, and fry for about 5 minutes, or until crisp and brown; drain on paper towels. When cool enough to handle, set aside ¼ cup oil; store the remaining oil for another use.

• Heat the reserved ¼ cup oil very hot in a frying pan. Add the carrot slices and fry over high heat for about 1 minute. Add the tofu, soybean sprouts, green onions, soy sauce, sugar, salt, and sesame oil, and stir-fry about 1 minute more. Taste and adjust the seasonings.

Makes 5 servings.

Steamed Coconut Tofu

⅔ lb (300 g) firm tofu
5 shallots
3 garlic cloves
2 small Indian bay leaves* (salam)
½ bunch chives
1 bunch cilantro*
3 red chilies
1 tablespoon brown sugar
2 tablespoons fresh lime juice
⅞ cup (200 ml) coconut milk
2 eggs
1½ teaspoons salt
¼ cup plus 1 tablespoon (35 g) grated coconut

*Preparation time:
about 1¼ hours*

Tofu with Soybean Sprouts

⅞ lb (400 g) firm tofu
1 medium-size carrot
generous ½ lb (250 g) soybean sprouts
2 green onions
1 quart (1 l) vegetable oil
scant ¼ cup (45 ml) light soy sauce*
2 tablespoons sugar
1 teaspoon salt
1 tablespoon sesame oil*

*Preparation time:
about 35 minutes*

PER SERVING:	274 CALORIES	
NUTRITIONAL INFORMATION		
Carbohydrate	13	g
Protein	14	g
Total fat	20	g
Cholesterol	85	mg
Sodium	743	mg
Fiber	3	g

PER SERVING:	378 CALORIES	
NUTRITIONAL INFORMATION		
Carbohydrate	15	g
Protein	15	g
Total fat	31	g
Cholesterol	0	mg
Sodium	2129	mg
Fiber	2	g

Tofu in Curry Sauce

2/3 lb (330 g) firm tofu
1 large green bell pepper
2 red chilies
2 medium-size onions
2 teaspoons cornstarch
5/8 cup (150 ml) vegetable oil
2 tablespoons medium-hot curry powder
1²/3 cups (400 ml) coconut milk
2 tablespoons sugar
1 teaspoon salt
2 tablespoons chili oil*
1³/4 oz (50 g) basil leaves* (bai horapha)

Preparation time: about 30 minutes

Spicy Fried Tofu

7/8 lb (400 g) firm tofu
2 small onions
2 (2-inch long) pieces fresh ginger*
4 garlic cloves
2 red chilies
1 teaspoon ground coriander
1 pinch laos*
scant 1/4 cup (54 g) brown sugar
1 Indian bay leaf* (salam)
1 teaspoon salt
2 tablespoons fresh lime juice
1/2 cup (120 ml) vegetable oil

Preparation time: about 1¹/4 hours

Tofu in Curry Sauce
From China • Pictured

• Rinse the tofu under cold running water, let drain, then cut into pieces about 2 inches (5 cm) long, 1/2 inch (2 cm) wide, and 1/8 inch (1/2 cm) thick.

• Halve the bell pepper, trim, and wash; cut into 1/2-inch- (1-cm)- wide strips. Wash the chilies, removing the stems; cut on the diagonal into rings. Peel and halve the onions, then cut them into thick slices. In a small bowl, stir cornstarch with 2 tablespoons water until smooth.

• Heat the oil in a frying pan. Add the tofu and fry over high heat for about 3 minutes. Add the curry powder and stir-fry briefly. Add the coconut milk, sugar, salt, bell pepper strips, chilies, and onions; let simmer for about 5 minutes, stirring occasionally. Stir in the chili oil and cornstarch mixture. Wash the basil leaves, then stir into the tofu mixture.

Makes 5 servings.

PER SERVING:	574 CALORIES	
NUTRITIONAL INFORMATION		
Carbohydrate	21	g
Protein	8	g
Total fat	54	g
Cholesterol	0	mg
Sodium	502	mg
Fiber	4	g

Spicy Fried Tofu
From Indonesia • Classic

• Rinse the tofu under cold running water; let drain, then cut into finger-length pieces about 1 inch (3 cm) wide and 1/2 inch (1 cm) thick. Peel and halve the onions, then cut them into thick slices. Peel and finely chop the ginger and garlic. Wash the chilies, removing the stems, then finely chop.

• In a large pot, combine tofu, onions, ginger, garlic, chilies, coriander, laos, sugar, bay leaf, salt, lime juice, and about 2 cups (1/2 l) of water. Bring to a boil and let cook, uncovered, until all the liquid has evaporated, about 40 minutes. Remove tofu pieces and let cool.

• Heat the oil in a frying pan until very hot. Add tofu and fry about 3 minutes, or until golden-brown. Serve immediately.

Makes 5 servings.

Tip
Serve the tofu with vegetable dishes and salads.

PER SERVING:	307 CALORIES	
NUTRITIONAL INFORMATION		
Carbohydrate	18	g
Protein	7	g
Total fat	24	g
Cholesterol	0	mg
Sodium	500	mg
Fiber	1	g

UNBEATABLE!

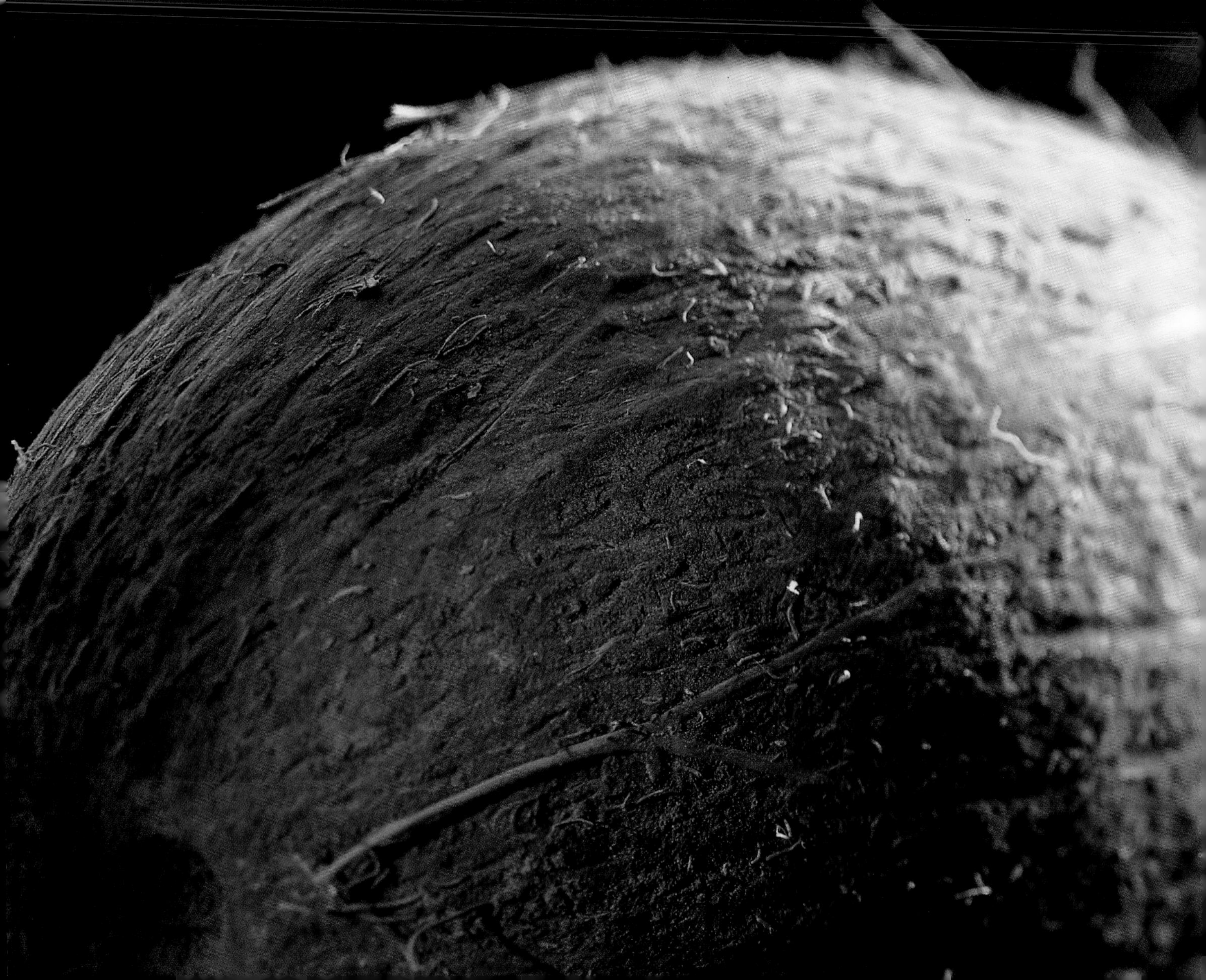

Rice and Noodle Dishes

The Reverence for Grain

In Asia, rice is at the center of every meal; without it a meal would not be complete. Rice is the most important basic food—comparable to bread and potatoes of the Western world. The day begins with rice at breakfast, it ends with rice at the evening meal, and rice must not be missing from the midday meal either.

In Asia, there are several varieties of rice. Since it plays such a large role in the diet, the demand for quality rice can be very high. So in Japan, there are special rice dealers who carry many rice varieties from different growing areas.

For those who live in the agricultural regions and work in the rice paddies, life is dictated by the growing seasons. Depending on the region, once, twice, or—in the case of Bali—three times a year, rice plants must be carefully planted individually by hand in the muddy ground. The rice is harvested again by hand. It's no wonder the Asians have a reverence for rice and don't waste a grain. Rice is a symbol of fertility—which is expressed in the West by the throwing of rice at weddings—nourishment, and life.

Often the Focal Point, Never a Side Issue

This versatile white grain can be prepared in many different ways: boiled in water or coconut milk, or fried or roasted.

Nasi goreng, fried rice with vegetables, spices, and fried eggs has been declared the national dish in Indonesia. Called fried rice here, it is a popular dish worldwide.

Rice can be served on the side with every possible dish, but rice often is the main dish, to which a variety of vegetables are added. However, in poorer regions, it also may be eaten with only fish sauce. Probably the most elaborate form in which rice is served is in Indonesia. A large group of people sits at a long table on which giant bowls of rice are placed. Thirty to forty side dishes are served with the rice, and the guests pass the food, family-style.

Rice for Your Own Cuisine

Good long-grain rice is available in any supermarket, but an Asian grocery might have a better selection. Thai fragrant rice (jasmine) is particularly good. It gives off a very appetizing aroma while cooking. This rice is always cooked without salt. The basic recipe is given on this page.

Also very popular in Asia is sticky rice. This rice traditionally is formed into little balls. The rice balls are then dipped into different sauces before being eaten. When preparing this rice, be sure to soak it in water overnight before steaming it. Rice is also ground into flour, which is used primarily for sweet dishes.

Noodles for Any Occasion

Noodles are the second most important food. There are numerous varieties, which differ greatly from one another in their composition and form. The noodle used for soup is different from the noodle used with a sauce. There are special varieties for boiling and for frying, particularly for deep-frying, and noodles that are to be eaten cold have an altogether different texture.

Basic Fragrant Rice

For 4 portions, thoroughly wash $1/2$ lb (250 g) jasmine rice under cold running water. Place the rice in a large pot, and cover it by $1/2$ inch (2 cm) with water. Cover the pot and bring to a boil. Take off the cover and reduce the heat. When the rice is simmering gently, replace the cover, and cook the rice for about 20 minutes, or until all the water has been absorbed by the rice.

Tip

When making fried rice, let the steamed rice cool completely, uncovered, preferably overnight, before stir-frying.

³/₄ lb (350 g) thin rice noodles
(such as vermicelli)
1¹/₈ lb (500 g) firm tofu
1 quart (1 l) vegetable oil
3 eggs
1¹/₂ teaspoon salt
¹/₃ lb (150 g) soybean sprouts
¹/₃ lb (150 g) young garlic
chives
2 hot red peppers
8 shallots
3³/₈ cups (800 ml) coconut
milk
¹/₄ cup (60 ml) bean sauce*
¹/₄ cup (70 g) sugar
¹/₄ cup plus 1 tablespoon
(74 ml) fresh lime juice
1 teaspoon chili powder

Preparation time:
about 40 minutes

Rice Noodles with Coconut Sauce

From Vietnam • Classic

• Place the rice noodles in a large bowl and cover with hot water; soften for about 20 minutes.

• Meanwhile, rinse the tofu under cold running water and let drain. Cut about two-thirds of the tofu into pieces about 1 inch (3 cm) long, ¹/₂ inch (1 cm) wide, and ¹/₈ inch (¹/₂ cm) thick. Mash the remaining tofu in a bowl with a fork.

• Heat the oil very hot in a large pot. Add the tofu pieces and fry until golden-brown, about 5 minutes. Remove tofu from the oil with a skimmer and drain on paper towels. When cool enough to handle, set aside ¹/₄ cup oil; store remaining oil for another use.

• Heat reserved ¹/₄ cup oil in a frying pan over medium heat. In a small bowl, whisk the eggs with ¹/₂ teaspoon salt, then pour egg mixture into the pan. Cook until set on one side, then turn. Fry the eggs 1 minute more, then remove from pan to cool on paper towels. Cut cooked eggs into thin strips.

• Wash the soybean sprouts and garlic chives. Cut the greens into 1¹/₂-inch-(4-cm)- long pieces. Wash the peppers, removing the stems; halve peppers lengthwise, then cut into strips. Peel and dice the shallots.

• Heat the coconut milk in a pot; add the shallots, and let simmer over medium heat for about 3 minutes. Stir in the mashed tofu, remaining salt, bean sauce, sugar, lime juice, and chili powder. Cook over low heat for about 1 minute. Pour half of the sauce into a bowl.

• Drain the rice noodles in a colander. Add the noodles to the rest of the sauce in the pot and heat on high for about 1 minute. Stir in the soybean sprouts, garlic chives, and fried tofu and cook to heat through.

• Arrange the noodle mixture on a serving plate, and garnish with the egg and pepper strips. Serve with the reserved sauce.

Makes 6 servings.

PER SERVING:	690 CALORIES	
NUTRITIONAL INFORMATION		
Carbohydrate	37	g
Protein	17	g
Total fat	57	g
Cholesterol	106	mg
Sodium	938	mg
Fiber	4	g

Rice Noodles with Hot Peppers

From Thailand • Pictured

- Bring a large pot of water to a boil. Add the noodles, and cook for about 4 minutes; pour noodles into a colander, rinse with cold water, and let drain.

- Wash and trim the oyster mushrooms, then coarsely chop. Peel and mince the garlic. Wash the hot peppers, removing the stems, then chop. Wash the basil; remove the leaves, discarding the stems.

- In a frying pan, heat the oil until very hot. Add the hot peppers and garlic, and fry over high heat for about 1 minute. Add the noodles, mushrooms, soy sauces, and sugar. Stir well to combine. Taste and adjust the seasonings with salt and sugar. Stir in the basil just before serving.

Makes 5 servings.

Fried Rice with Peanuts

From Vietnam • Easy to prepare

- Peel and mince the garlic. Wash the hot peppers, removing the stems, then finely chop. Wash and trim the green onions, then cut into thin slices, including delicate green tops.

- Heat the oil in a frying pan. Add the garlic and fry until golden-brown. Add the hot peppers and peanuts, and fry briefly. Add the green onions, cooked rice, soy sauce, salt, sugar, and lime juice, then fry for about 1 minute, until the rice is heated through.

Makes 5 servings.

Tip

Serve different vegetables with this rice dish (for example, cauliflower with chilies, see page 36, or oyster mushrooms with basil, see page 33).

(for example, cauliflower with chilies, see page 36, or oyster mushrooms with basil, see page 33).

PER SERVING:	349 CALORIES
NUTRITIONAL INFORMATION	
Carbohydrate 44	g
Protein 7	g
Total fat 14	g
Cholesterol 0	mg
Sodium 1092	mg
Fiber 3	g

PER SERVING:	387 CALORIES
NUTRITIONAL INFORMATION	
Carbohydrate 48	g
Protein 8	g
Total fat 18	g
Cholesterol 0	mg
Sodium 949	mg
Fiber 2	g

Rice Noodles with Hot Peppers

1/2 lb (200 g) rice noodles (1/4 to 1/2 inch/1 to 2 cm wide)
1/2 lb (200 g) oyster mushrooms
5 garlic cloves
2 hot red peppers
1/4 lb (100 g) red Thai basil* (bai grapau)
1/4 cup plus 1 tablespoon vegetable oil
scant 1/4 cup light soy sauce*
1 tablespoon dark soy sauce*
2 tablespoons sugar
salt

Preparation time: about 25 minutes

Fried Rice with Peanuts

4 garlic cloves
2 hot red peppers
2 green onions
1/4 cup plus 1 tablespoon vegetable oil
generous 1/2 cup (100 g) roasted, salted peanuts
1 2/3 lb (750 g) cooked rice (from 1 heaping cup/250 g raw rice)
1/4 cup (60 ml) light soy sauce*
1/2 teaspoon salt
2 tablespoons sugar
scant 1/4 cup (45 ml) fresh lime juice

Preparation time: about 20 minutes

5 shiitake mushrooms*
generous ¹/₂ lb (250 g) egg
noodles (such as bamie)
¹/₂ lb (200 g) spinach
¹/₂ cup (50 g) soybean sprouts
1 large carrot
3 garlic cloves
¹/₂ cup (120 ml) vegetable oil
2 tablespoons sugar
2 tablespoons light soy sauce*
1 teaspoon salt
freshly ground black pepper

Preparation time:
35 minutes

Fried Noodles with Spinach
From China • Classic

• Place the shiitake mushrooms in a bowl and cover with warm water; soften for about 20 minutes.

• Meanwhile, bring a large pot of water to a boil. Add the noodles, and cook about 3 minutes; pour into a colander, rinse briefly with cold water, then let drain.

• Pick over the spinach and wash in several changes of cold water. Wash the soybean sprouts. Drain spinach and sprouts. Trim and peel the carrot, then cut lengthwise into slices; cut the slices into matchsticks. Peel and mince the garlic.

• Drain the mushrooms in a colander then cut into thin strips.

• Heat the oil in a frying pan or wok over high heat. Add the garlic and fry, stirring, until golden-brown. Add the noodles, carrot slices, and mushrooms, then fry for about 1 minute. Add the spinach, soybean sprouts, sugar, soy sauce, and salt. Fry over high heat for about 1 more minute, stirring constantly. Season the noodles with ground black pepper and serve.

Makes 5 servings.

Tip
Place little bowls of chili powder and sugar on the table so that each person can season to his or her own taste.

PER SERVING:	427 CALORIES	
NUTRITIONAL INFORMATION		
Carbohydrate	45	g
Protein	10	g
Total fat	24	g
Cholesterol	43	mg
Sodium	929	mg
Fiber	3	g

Nasi Goreng
From Indonesia • Pictured

• Heat the oil in a large pot. Meanwhile, peel and halve the onions, then cut them into thin slices. Fry the onion slices in the hot oil until crispy and golden-brown; remove from the oil with a skimmer, and drain on paper towels. When cool enough to handle, set aside ¹/₂ cup oil, storing the remaining oil for another use.

• Peel and finely chop the shallots. Peel the chilies, removing the stems, and finely chop. In a large frying pan or wok, heat ¹/₄ cup of the reserved oil. Add the shallots and chilies, and stir-fry for about 1 minute. Add the rice, ketchup, teriyaki sauce, salt, paprika, and sugar, and heat, stirring constantly; set aside.

• Heat remaining ¹/₄ cup of oil in another frying pan. Break the eggs separately into the oil and fry them to desired doneness. Divide the rice among 4 plates; place 1 fried egg on each portion of rice, and sprinkle onions over top. Garnish with cilantro leaves.

Makes 4 servings.

PER SERVING:	670 CALORIES	
NUTRITIONAL INFORMATION		
Carbohydrate	64	g
Protein	13	g
Total fat	40	g
Cholesterol	212	mg
Sodium	902	mg
Fiber	3	g

Cold White Noodles
From Japan • Refreshing

• Bring a large pot of water to a boil. Add somen, and cook according to the package directions; pour into a colander and let drain.

• For the sauce, peel the ginger and grate it into a bowl; add the soy sauce and mix. Add the vegetable broth, sugar, and mirin and stir carefully; set aside.

• Place 4 or 5 ice cubes in a dishcloth and pound with a mallet or heavy object. Pour the noodles into a serving bowl; distribute the crushed ice over top. Garnish the noodles with lime slices, maraschino cherries, and mint leaves. Serve the sauce on the side.

Makes 4 servings.

Tip
Vegetable Tempura (see page 40) goes especially well with Cold White Noodles.

PER SERVING:	488 CALORIES	
NUTRITIONAL INFORMATION		
Carbohydrate	104	g
Protein	15	g
Total fat	1	g
Cholesterol	0	mg
Sodium	4283	mg
Fiber	5	g

Nasi Goreng
1 cup (¹/₄ l) vegetable oil
2 large onions
5 shallots
3 red chilies
1 ²/₃ lb (750 g) cooked rice
(from 1 heaping cup/250 g
raw rice)
1 tablespoon ketchup
2 tablespoons teriyaki sauce
¹/₂ teaspoon salt
1 teaspoon Hungarian
paprika
1 teaspoon sugar
4 eggs

For garnish:
cilantro leaves*

Preparation time:
about 20 minutes

Cold White Noodles
scant 1 lb (400 g) somen
(white Japanese noodles)
2 (2-inch) pieces fresh ginger*
¹/₂ cup (¹/₈ l) Japanese soy
sauce*
¹/₂ cup (¹/₈ l) vegetable broth
(see page 9)
2 tablespoons sugar
¹/₄ cup (60 ml) mirin*

For garnish:
lime slices
maraschino cherries
mint leaves, rinsed

Preparation time:
about 25 minutes

Fried Rice with Vegetables

3 garlic cloves
5 shallots
1 cup (150 g) soybean sprouts
2 medium-size carrots
1 cup (150 g) sugar-snap peas
3 eggs
1 1/2 teaspoons salt
1/2 cup (120 ml) vegetable oil
1 2/3 lb (750 g) cooked rice
(from 1 heaping cup/250 g
raw rice)
2 tablespoons ketchup
1 tablespoon sugar
2 teaspoons sambal oelek
(see page 27)
2 tablespoons teriyaki sauce

Preparation time:
about 30 minutes

Fried Rice with Pineapple

1 small pineapple
(about 1 1/4 lb/600 g)
1 (12-oz/340-g) can whole-
kernel corn
1 medium-size red bell pepper
1/2 cup (50 g) raisins
4 garlic cloves
1/2 cup (120 ml) vegetable oil
2 eggs
1/2 cup (100 g) frozen peas
1 2/3 lb (750 g) cooked rice
(from 1 heaping cup/250 g
raw rice)
1/4 cup plus 1 tablespoon
light soy sauce*
2 teaspoons sugar
1 teaspoon salt

Preparation time:
about 25 minutes

Fried Rice with Vegetables

From Indonesia • Easy to prepare

• Peel and finely chop the garlic and shallots. Rinse the soybean sprouts in cold water and let drain. Trim and peel the carrots, then cut into matchsticks. Wash the peas and trim the ends.

• Whisk the eggs with 1/2 teaspoon salt in a bowl. Heat 3 tablespoons oil in a frying pan over medium heat. Add the eggs, and fry until set and golden-brown on both sides. Cut the omelet into strips.

• Heat the remaining oil in a frying pan. Add the garlic and shallots and fry for about 2 minutes. Add the carrots, sugar-snap peas, and soybean sprouts, and fry for about 2 minutes. Stir in the rice, then stir in the remaining salt, ketchup, sugar, sambal oelek, and teriyaki sauce. Stir-fry for about 2 more minutes. Stir in the omelet strips and serve immediately.

Makes 5 servings.

PER SERVING:	498 CALORIES	
NUTRITIONAL INFORMATION		
Carbohydrate	55	g
Protein	11	g
Total fat	26	g
Cholesterol	127	mg
Sodium	1229	mg
Fiber	2	g

Fried Rice with Pineapple

From Thailand • Pictured

• Peel the pineapple; halve lengthwise and remove the core. Cut the pineapple into bite-size chunks. Pour corn into a colander to drain.

• Wash and halve the pepper; remove seeds and dice. In a small bowl, plump the raisins in hot water; let drain. Peel and mince the garlic.

• Heat 1/4 cup oil to very hot in a frying pan. Add the eggs, stir, and cook until set; divide eggs into large pieces, and push to one side. Add the remaining oil to the pan. When hot, add garlic and stir-fry until golden-brown. Stir garlic into the eggs.

• Add the pineapple, bell pepper, corn, raisins, peas, and rice. Stir-fry for about 2 minutes. Season to taste with soy sauce, sugar, and salt.

Makes 5 servings.

PER SERVING:	608 CALORIES	
NUTRITIONAL INFORMATION		
Carbohydrate	90	g
Protein	11	g
Total fat	25	g
Cholesterol	85	mg
Sodium	1542	mg
Fiber	5	g

Rice with Flower Mushrooms

1/2 cup (70 g) dried flower
mushrooms*
2 medium-size carrots
4 garlic cloves
1/2 cup (120 ml) vegetable oil
1/2 cup (100 g) frozen peas
1 2/3 lb (750 g) cooked rice
scant 1/4 cup (45 ml) light soy
sauce*
1 teaspoon salt
2 tablespoons sugar
generous 1/2 cup (100 g) roasted
cashews
1 teaspoon sesame oil*

*Preparation time:
about 30 minutes
(+ 1 hour soaking time)*

Curried Noodles with Peppers

generous 1/2 lb (250 g) egg
noodles (mieh)
2 stalks lemongrass*
2 (2-inch) pieces fresh ginger*
1 each, medium-size: red and
green bell peppers
1/4 cup plus 1 tablespoon
(75 ml) vegetable oil
1/2 teaspoon turmeric*
1 teaspoon ground coriander
1 teaspoon sambal oelek
(see page 27)
1/2 teaspoon Hungarian paprika
scant 1/4 cup (45 ml) teriyaki
sauce
1 teaspoon salt
1 2/3 cups (400 ml) coconut milk

*Preparation time:
about 40 minutes*

92

Rice with Flower Mushrooms

From China • More time-consuming

• Place flower mushrooms in a bowl and cover with warm water; let soak for about 1 hour. Pour the mushrooms into a colander to drain, then cut into bite-size pieces.

• Bring about 2 cups (1/2 l) water to a boil in a large pot. Trim and peel the carrots; cut into 1/2 inch (1 cm) cubes. Add carrots to boiling water, and blanch for about 2 minutes; drain in a colander.

• Peel and mince the garlic. Heat the oil in a frying pan until very hot. Add the garlic and fry until golden-brown. Add the mushrooms, carrots, peas, and rice, then fry about 1 minute.

• Add the soy sauce, salt, sugar, cashews, and sesame oil; mix well, and serve immediately.

Makes 5 servings.

PER SERVING:	519 CALORIES	
NUTRITIONAL INFORMATION		
Carbohydrate	55	g
Protein	11	g
Total fat	30	g
Cholesterol	0	mg
Sodium	3787	mg
Fiber	4	g

Curried Noodles with Peppers

From Indonesia • Pictured

• Bring 2 quarts (2 l) water to boil in a large pot. Add the noodles and cook according to the package directions, but do not overcook. Pour noodles into a colander and briefly run under cold water; let drain.

• Wash the lemongrass; cut into thin slices, then finely chop. Peel and finely chop the ginger. Halve the peppers; remove the seeds and white membranes. Rinse the peppers, then cut into strips.

• Heat the oil very hot in a large frying pan or wok. Add the lemongrass, ginger, pepper strips, turmeric, coriander, sambel oelek, paprika, teriyaki sauce, and salt, and fry for about 2 minutes. Stir in the noodles and stir-fry over high heat for about 2 minutes. Pour in the coconut milk, and let simmer for about 1 minute more.

Makes 5 servings.

PER SERVING:	485 CALORIES	
NUTRITIONAL INFORMATION		
Carbohydrate	44	g
Protein	10	g
Total fat	32	g
Cholesterol	43	mg
Sodium	1311	mg
Fiber	5	g

INDEX

See the inside front cover for Asian Cooking Tools, and see the inside back cover for Traditional Asian Ingredients.